Stock Market for Beginners Book:
Stock Market Basics Explained for Beginners Investing in the Stock Market

Evan J. Houpt & John Border

First Print Edition

Disclaimer: This book contains general information regarding finance and investment that is based on the author's own knowledge and experiences. It is published for general reference and is not intended to be a substitute for the advice of a financial professional or accountant. The publisher and the author disclaim any personal liability, either directly or indirectly, for the information contained within. Although the author and the publisher have made every effort to ensure the accuracy and completeness of the information presented here, they assume no responsibility for errors, inaccuracies, omissions and inconsistencies.

To Nedra,

Through Thick and Thin – Evan Houpt

To Michelle Border

*For Listening patiently to stock market
stories all these years – John Border*

Table of Contents

Introduction

I have always had an interest in business and investing. During my years as an engineer for one of the Big Three automakers, I began to pay attention to the financial markets and started faithfully reading the *Wall Street Journal*. When the internet started making information about the stock market accessible to ordinary people, I started reading the online financial gurus. In fact, I still believe that online stock charts are the greatest thing to happen in the financial marketplace since the New York Stock Exchange opened its doors.

This book is written for the retail investor who wants an overview of the market in easily understandable terms and a clear explanation of how the pieces fit together. My goal is to leave you with a practical working knowledge of the stock market with a minimum cost of time and frustration when you finish this book.

I don't recommend particular stocks, and other than some time-tested strategies that every investor should know, I don't recommend a particular technique or philosophy. That's because I don't follow financial gurus, and in my opinion, you shouldn't either. I do include some methods from the experts in Chapter 6, but only so you can compare different approaches and examine them with a critical eye. My first accountant told me, "Evan, nobody cares about your money as much as you do." That advice has stayed with me and spurred me to keep learning. Knowledge is power – power that allows me to maintain complete control over my investments and not be taken in by the latest and greatest investment fad without examining it for myself and seeing whether it passes the smell test.

When I took an early retirement from my job nine years ago, I knew I wanted to try my hand at the stock market. I had a nice retirement package and years of savings built up. My wife, Nedra, and I owned our home free and clear. Our children were grown and their college was nearly paid for. The United States economy was doing decently. So I bought a couple of books on stock investing and became a retail investor.

I know you're thinking, "What's next?" You're wondering if I figured out how to beat the market and became a millionaire. Or the more pessimistic of you are wondering if I bet our life savings on a dud IPO and lost everything.

The answer is neither. I didn't figure out how to beat the market, although I wasted a lot of time and energy trying to. And I didn't bet the farm on my stock investments. Even if I had been dumb enough to do that, Nedra would have brought me up short in a big hurry.

The biggest challenge for me over the past nine years was simplifying the process. I've read numerous books for beginning stock investors, and too few of them do a good job of explaining the big picture and where someone like you or me fits in. Plenty of books define investment terms like market cap, ETFs, and IRAs, but understanding those terms in isolation from each other didn't help me one bit. In my confusion, combined with my engineer's tendency to overcomplicate things, I made a few beginner's mistakes and worried far more than I needed to before making a decision.

But I persevered and learned, partly by studying, and partly by doing. I invested very conservatively and did a lot of practice investing on simulator websites until I felt more confident. As I learned more, I discovered that my background as an engineer gave me an advantage, and I found myself applying my analytical and math skills in a new way. Investing became fun and emotionally rewarding, as well as bringing me excellent financial returns.

Apply what you learn here to develop your own investment style. Be creative and enjoy the process. Don't spend more time or money than you have, and if you find yourself worrying about your investments, remember that even the world's greatest investors often call it wrong.

I wish you happiness and prosperity – in equal and generous quantities.

– Evan Houpt

Chapter 1
Investment Options

Stocks are a great way to invest your income and receive a return, but they're not the only way. When I first started investing, I was entirely focused on stocks and made that choice without looking at the alternatives. Fortunately, I'm happy with my results, but if I had a do-over, I would compare stocks next to other investment vehicles and make a more informed decision.

To keep you from starting out with the disadvantage I had, let's look at the big picture of stocks.

Understanding Securities

To understand stocks, you should know what securities are, because a stock is a type of security. A security is a financial instrument that has a certain monetary value and is *fungible* – meaning that it can be purchased or traded. As an investor, securities are your bread and butter – you invest in them, and if you invest well, they give you a return on your investment in the form of interest, growth, or dividends – or sometimes a combination of these three.

Securities may be private, which means only select individuals may invest in them, or they may be public, meaning that anyone can invest in them as long as they're willing to follow the rules that govern investors and investments. In the United States, the rules for publicly traded securities are set and enforced by the Securities and Exchange Commission (SEC). It is the job of the SEC to make sure that investors are treated fairly, and that all investments are presented honestly and free of illegal dealings such as insider trading.

There are two types of securities: equity securities and debt securities. Here are some facts about each type.

Equity Securities

Equity securities are ownership interests in a company that issues them and allows them to be publicly traded on the open market. Because the owner of the equity security actually owns a piece of the company, he gets part of the company's profit or loss.

A stock is the most common type of equity security. Stocks are sometimes simply called "equities." Stock owners are called "shareholders," because they hold a share of the company.

Why Stocks Are a Great Investment

There are some excellent reasons that the stock market is so attractive to investors:

- On the average, returns from stocks outpace the inflation rate of US currency, coming in at above 10 percent annually, compared to an inflation rate of just over 3 percent.

- The tax rates for the returns on most stocks are lower than for other investments (see Chapter 10, Managing Your Tax Liabilities).

- Liquidity. Although liquidating your stock portfolio to raise emergency funds isn't the best financial management strategy, sometimes it's necessary, and when you own stocks, converting them to cash is a simple matter of calling your broker.

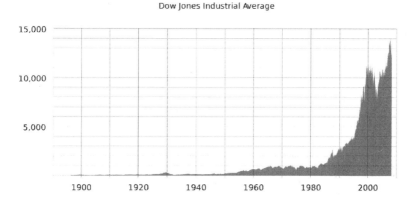

Dow Jones Industrial Average

Chart showing growth of the Dow Jones Industrial Average since 1900 (not adjusted for inflation)

The down side of stock investment is that there's some risk. That's not surprising. Generally, in life as well as in the investment world, risk and reward tend to go hand in hand. The up side is that a good diversification strategy and smart decisions can mitigate most of the risk

Stock Classes

There are two types, or classes, of stocks you should be familiar with.

- **Preferred stock** is a higher class of stock than common stock and provides extra benefits to the shareholder. Preferred stock holders often receive an extra return on their shares, called dividends. If the company goes out of business, preferred shareholders are paid first. However, preferred shares usually don't include voting rights. Some preferred stocks are classified as debt securities instead of as equities because their terms are so restrictive.

- **Common stock** is a single class of shares, usually the largest class in the company. Some common stock pays dividends (see Chapters 8 and 9), but only after the preferred shareholders take theirs. Holders of common stock are the last to be paid for their shares in a liquidation. Common stock holders always have voting

15

rights. As a retail investor, you'll almost always be investing in common stock.

The Responsibilities of Stock Ownership

Although the rise of discount brokerages and the wealth of information on the market has made it easy to get into the stock market, the responsibility of managing your stock portfolio ultimately falls on you. When you sign a brokerage agreement, you'll see in the fine print that you don't get to blame your broker if the market takes a turn for the worse and you lose money on your investments. Even a mutual fund, which is about as hands-off an investment vehicle as you can get, should get scrutiny by you on a quarterly or monthly basis to make sure you're not wasting your money in the wrong investments.

Now, about voting rights. When you buy stock in a company, you're a co-owner, so you receive the right to vote on large issues that affect the company. You get one vote for each share you own, so the more shares you own, the more your vote influences the company.

The largest issue before you as a holder of common stock in a company is voting for the board of directors. The board is the decision-making body of the company and is responsible for hiring and firing upper management, as well as major investment decisions such as mergers and buyouts. Sometimes shareholders also vote on very large matters of company policy, including compensation of executives. However, the business judgment decisions for the day-to-day operations of the company are in the hands of the board and the upper level managers.

Many individual shareholders don't vote their shares because they believe their votes don't matter if they only own a small percentage of the company's stock. I always vote my shares because it's so easy, and I believe that if enough people vote, it makes a difference. Voting your shares doesn't require you to travel to corporate headquarters. If you're a shareholder, the company is required by law to send you a proxy voting statement, either electronically or by mail. Your vote is through a "proxy," a real person who casts votes on your behalf as you direct him or her. You can vote online, or by filling out and mailing back your proxy statement.

Shareholders can sell their stocks to other people, and they can buy stocks from other people. That's called trading. That's what this book is about, and that's where the fun begins.

Other Equity Securities

There are other ways besides stocks for you to invest your funds and own a part of your investment. For example, a money market fund is one type of mutual fund that's about as simple as it gets if you are looking for an entry level route into investing in equities. Like other mutual funds, money market funds are sold by financial management firms. Unlike stocks and ordinary mutual funds, shares of a money market fund have a fixed price, normally $1 per share. These funds pay out dividends, and they're fairly liquid, so you can make withdrawals on short notice.

Additional equity securities, like real estate, partnerships, and owning your own business can provide handsome returns. However, lack of liquidity plagues these other equity investments. You shouldn't pursue them unless you're comfortable with having your money tied up for months or years at a time.

Debt Securities

Debt securities are interests in a loan that a borrower agrees to repay to a lender, with interest. The original loan will have clearly defined terms for the borrower and lender. These include:

- **Principal:** This is the original amount of the loan. If a borrower asks a lender for a loan of $500,000 to start a business, that amount is the principal.

- **Interest rate:** This is the percentage of the principal that gets added on to the loan to compensate the lender for

17

letting the borrower use his money. Interest rates are usually expressed as an annual percentage rate (APR), so an APR of 10 percent on a $500,000 loan would add $50,000 per year to the loan amount until the borrower starts paying it back.

- **Maturity date:** This is the date on which the loan must be paid back. For example, that 30-year mortgage on your home means you must repay the principal plus any accrued interest in full within 30 years after you signed the mortgage note.

Debt securities return income on your investment in the form of interest, as a reward for you lending out your money. They tend to be more stable than equity securities because you're virtually guaranteed to make back the principal. Retail investors are drawn to debt securities because of their simplicity along with their lower risk. These investments are typically sold through channels that provide a fair amount of hand holding for the rookie investor.

The trade off you make when you invest in debt securities is their lower return on your investment. A good rule of thumb you should learn up front with investing is that low risk means a lower return, while higher risk brings a higher return. Because the borrower has to pay back the principal no matter what, the interest rate on the loan is low and the lender makes less money than if he invested in the riskier arena of the stock market.

If you invest in debt securities, your relationship with the borrower will vary, depending on the type of security you're dealing with. With some types, such as bonds, you are the lender and have a direct relationship with the borrower. With other types, such as collateralized securities, the investor is not the original lender and never meets the borrower. Instead, an investment bank will make a deal with the lender to turn the original loan into securities that can be bought and sold in the financial marketplace. The investor in the collateralized security buys a chunk of this loan (called a tranche), and probably many others as well, in one package. The idea is to spread the risk of the individual debt securities among as many investors as possible. (See Chapter 10, Spotlight: The 2008 Collapse of the Financial Market and the Fate of the Big Banks.)

Collateralized securities are generally only offered to sophisticated private investors, such as hedge funds. If you're going to invest in debt securities, your only real choices are bonds, and certificates of deposit (CDs).

Bonds

The most common example of debt securities is bonds. Although the stock market gets the lion's share of attention from investors and the media because its returns are higher, I would be doing you, the reader, a disservice if I left bonds out of this book. Why? Because traditionally, bonds have been the safe harbor that investors look to when the stock market gets too volatile to invest all of their money in.

Bonds are subject to market forces just like stock, so they do fluctuate in price, but these fluctuations aren't nearly as extreme as the stock market can be. Some bonds, such as U.S. Savings Bonds can also be packaged into mutual funds (see Chapter 4, How Stocks Are Traded) to add diversity and stability for investors who prefer to have a fund manager build their portfolio instead of doing it themselves.

Here is some terminology for you to get familiar with if you're thinking of adding bonds to your investment portfolio:

- **Issuer:** The borrower is called the issuer, because it "issues" the bond, meaning it creates the loan as a debt security that can be publicly traded. Bonds can be issued by private corporations, by the federal government, and by state governments and municipalities such as cities and townships (these are called "muni bonds"). Government and muni issued bonds provide the investor with some significant tax advantages (see Chapter 10, Looking Toward the Future).

19

- **Bond Principal:** The principal amount of the bond is sometimes also called the "face value" (or sometimes the "par value") and is usually the purchase price of the bond, unless the issuer sells it to you at a discount. When you buy a bond, you're agreeing to lend the issuer the face value amount of the bond for a set period, such as five years.

- **Maturity:** Bonds are sold with a clearly defined maturity period. When this period ends, the bond issuer's obligation also ends, and it returns your investment to you. Bond maturity periods can range from 90 days for short-term federal treasury bills (called T-bills), to 30 years for long-term government bonds. Corporate bonds generally mature in three to 10 years.

- **Coupon:** The interest you receive when you invest in bonds is called the coupon rate, or sometimes just coupon. Until the bond matures, the issuer will calculate a fixed or variable interest rate on the principal and pay it out to you at intervals, usually six months.

- **Yield:** This is the measurement method for calculating the money you make on your bond investment. Yields are calculated in two ways. The *current yield* is coupon income only, which is calculated similar to the yield on dividends (see Chapter 8, Introduction to Dividend Investing). Current yield measures the ratio of a bond's price to its annual coupon and is always expressed as a percentage. The formula for calculating yield is: *annual coupon / bond price* For example, if you pay $85 for a bond with a $4 annual coupon ($2 every six months), your current yield is about 4.7% ($4 / $85). The *maturity yield* takes the coupon yield and adds in any appreciation in the bond principal if you purchased it at a discount.

The thing to remember about bonds is that in a volatile market, their prices tend to go up because more investors are seeking a more stable investment vehicle, so the demand increases their purchase price. At the same time, as the demand and price for bonds goes up, the yield, or interest payout, goes down.

Bonds are rated according to how much risk they present. The major rating agencies are Moody's, Standard and Poor's, and Fitch Ratings. Their classification labels are pretty similar, though not quite identical, and are designed to tell investors about the bond issuer's credit status. Good credit earns the issuer investment-grade status on its bonds, which the raters label AAA, AA, A, or BBB (Moody's calls BBB status Baa). Poor credit results in junk-bond status, labeled BB (Moody's calls this Ba), B, CCC, CC, C, and D. D in this case also stands for default status.

Generally, bonds aren't a very liquid investment vehicle. When you buy a bond, you're in for the duration of the maturity period, with the exception of some US Treasury bonds that are traded on exchanges just like stocks. You can also make bond investments all or part of your mutual fund portfolio to give you greater liquidity if that's important to you.

Corporate Bonds

Corporations issue their own bonds and traditionally, they were considered very good investments – similar to dividends (see Chapters 8 and 9), but with higher yields. However, corporate bonds do have risk, especially in today's volatile economy. For one thing, most corporate bonds are issued without collateral, so you're depending on the company's credit status and the integrity of the rating agencies when you evaluate their risk.

The other drawback of corporate bonds is that some of them are callable. This means that the issuing company can pay you back your principal before you've had the chance to collect all of your coupon payments for the full maturity period.

Government and Municipal Bonds

The US government issues bonds to raise funds for the expense of running the government, and for special projects. States and municipalities also issue bonds, called "muni's." It would beyond the scope of this book to describe all of the different types of government bonds and their ins and outs. Suffice to say that US Treasury bonds are considered extremely stable because if the fed defaults, we're all in a world of trouble!

However, municipal bonds aren't as attractive as they were before the recent financial crisis. The twenty-first century has seen several major US cities declare bankruptcy, putting the repayment of their bond obligations in jeopardy.

Before you invest in any bonds, evaluate the issuer as carefully as you would evaluate a company's stock.

Certificates of Deposit (CDs)

These debt securities are explained in more detail in Chapter 2, Setting and Reaching Your Investment Goals. Briefly, a CD is a loan you make directly to your bank, which pays you interest for the loan. There is usually a penalty if you try to withdraw your CD loan before the maturity date. CDs that offer you instant withdrawals generally pay a very low interest rate.

SPOTLIGHT: THE DETROIT BANKRUPTCY OF 2013 AND THE FATE OF THE MUNI BOND

One of Ernest Hemingway's fictional characters, when asked how he went bankrupt, replied: "Two ways. Gradually, then suddenly." The same can be said for the city of Detroit, which filed for Chapter 9 municipal bankruptcy on July 18, 2013. Formerly a major American urban center with a population of 1.8 million in 1950, it has since lost 60 percent of its residents. The city suffered from a declining tax base and periods of corruption and mismanagement, including an infamous former mayor currently serving a 20-year sentence in a federal prison for extortion, racketeering, and bribery. At the time of the filing, Detroit listed outstanding debt of $18 billion – the largest municipal bankruptcy in US history.

As Detroit's municipal bankruptcy filing became more and more likely, rumors began swirling around the US municipal bond market. Bonds in general have always been considered a very safe investment, and "muni bonds" issued by state and local government entities were once thought of as some of the safest bond investments on the market. But that was before Detroit's emergency manager Kevyn Orr, who took over management of the city under state law in early 2013 and later oversaw the bankruptcy filing, proposed to "rewrite" the Motor City's general obligation (GO) muni bonds to raise cash to satisfy other creditors in the bankruptcy. Orr has claimed that Detroit's muni bond holders wouldn't suffer any losses in the rewrite, but the investors protested loudly anyway. Rewriting an entire class of bonds that are normally considered investment grade would be a first in US investment history, and Wall Street has no desire to see volatility introduced into what was formerly considered a rock-solid investment vehicle. Supporters of Orr's plan countered that Detroit's muni bonds had been lowered to junk status years ago, and any bondholder who still held them when the bankruptcy was filed knew exactly what they were getting into. As of fall 2013, the fate of these bonds was still up in the air and may ultimately be decided by the bankruptcy court judge.

So, did the predictions of gloom and doom in 2013 for the muni bond market come true? Not exactly. Granted, other old industrial cities, particularly in the Midwest, or with less-than-stellar bond ratings, have actually delayed issuing new bonds since Detroit filed for Chapter 9, citing the difficulty of getting a good price for them due to investors' perception of the risk involved.

However, cities in solid financial shape with investment-grade bond status are still selling bonds, albeit for somewhat lower prices than in the past. Bond prices in general took an initial dip in early 2013, but the price of muni bonds has actually gone back *up* slightly in the wake of the Detroit bankruptcy. Seeing this small jump, many financial gurus encouraged investors to pick up some muni's while prices remained low and interest yields stayed high. I have added a few of them to my own portfolio, after first conducting a close scrutiny of the city's management and financial stability. Most muni bonds sport "triple tax-free" status – that is, their interest earnings are exempt from federal taxes, as well as the state and local taxes in the state and locality where they are issued – making them a tempting investment vehicle (see Chapter 10, Looking Toward the Future).

Another intriguing bond investment opportunity is to try to find non-GO types of muni bonds. GO bonds are sold without any asset backing, relying on the municipality's taxing power and general credit rating to support the belief that it will repay its investors. Remember, though, that GOs only comprise about 40 percent of the muni marketplace. Here are two non-GO options if you want to get started in the muni market while avoiding GO bonds:

- **Corporate-backed muni's:** A growing number of muni bonds are sold with corporate backing, rather than as GOs. Historically, muni's have paid out about 25 percent less interest than corporate bonds, but under unusual circumstances when their yields are about equal, as they were in mid-2013, the tax-free advantage of the muni paired with corporate backing is attractive to investors.

- **Project-backed muni's:** A second non-GO muni bond option is to look for muni's backed by specific projects that have a favorable debt-to-income ratio. City services, such as water and sewer systems, tend to earn nice revenues, since everyone needs them and the municipality has the option of raising the rates it charges to its residents. Public filings show that Detroit's water and sewer systems, for example, had about $406.3 million in total net revenue in fiscal year 2012, while only spending $356.6 million on debt payments, making their bondholders very happy indeed. Emergency Manager Orr saw an opportunity and proposed to sell off the systems to a regional authority, which would lease them back to the city before repaying bondholders. He also hoped to "rewrite" the water and sewer bonds as he tried to do with the GO bonds. However, he would need to get permission from the water and sewer system bondholders, who, unlike the GO bondholders, enjoy special protection under the federal bankruptcy code. The financial press reported that, not surprisingly, these specially protected bondholders showed little interest in agreeing to Orr's proposal.

Chapter 2
Setting and Reaching Your Investment Goals

I entered the stock market with advantages many other investors don't have. I had a solid pension plan, my wife and I owned our home free and clear, and saving for our children's college education was no longer a concern. Fortunately, we had steered clear of the enormous consumer debt that tempted so many people in the period between 2000 and 2008. We had set our financial goals years ago, and we were simply carrying them out.

You might not be in the same position as we were, so I want to emphasize how important it is to know where your money is, where it currently goes, and where it has to go over the next 20 years. Stock investment is a long-term commitment, and short-term thinking will get you short-term results – and those results might not be good.

Evaluating Your Investment Needs

The way you tailor your investment plan will depend on many factors. They include:

- **Your age.** Generally, the older you are, the less risk you will want to take with your investments, since you will have less time to make up for any losses.

- **Free time.** As a retiree, I have plenty of time to research my investments and put in the time it takes to build up my own portfolio. If you are still working, or your children are still at home, you have more demands on your time and will have less of it available for financial management.

- **Ability.** If you have a difficult time with numbers and financial concepts, then you will have to work harder to manage your own investments. But please don't think you need to be a born financial wizard to buy your own stocks. Investment skills are learnable if you arm yourself with good information, as I do, and have the desire to learn. Which brings us to the fourth factor...

- **Enthusiasm.** You need to enjoy the financial game in order to do well in it. If the subject of money bores you to tears, you will never commit yourself to the degree it takes to succeed in the market.

Take a look at your current position, both financially and personally. Be sure to involve your spouse or domestic partner in the decision making process if you aren't single. Start by evaluating your *time horizon*, which is the number of years you have to earn on your investments before you will need the money to live on in retirement. The longer your time horizon, the more aggressive you can be in your stock market investments. By "aggressive" I don't mean you should get into day trading or build your entire portfolio with high-risk, high-return stocks. Aggressive investment in this case means you can shift the balance of your portfolio toward equities, primarily stocks, and away from fixed-income vehicles such as bonds. As your time horizon shrinks, that balance should reverse, and you will end up with a larger number of fixed-income products and fewer equities over time.

Your next step is to get a clear view of your financial picture, if you haven't already. I use a spreadsheet program to make things go faster, but good old pencil and paper work equally well. You will be creating two pairs of worksheets.

The first pair of numbers is your income vs. your expenses:

- **Income.** On the first worksheet, list all of your income – net wages and tips after taxes, tax refunds, income from interest on investments you already have, and any annuities or inheritances. (If you are divorced and have full custody of your children, any child support income should match the expenses you incur in raising your children shown on the next worksheet, since this income is required to be spent for the children's benefit.) Calculate an annual figure and then divide it by 12 for the monthly average.

- **Expenses.** Start a new worksheet and do the same things with your expenses as you did for your income. Include mortgage payments, car payments, child support payments to an ex-spouse, revolving debt payments such as credit cards, income tax payments, utilities such as heating/cooling, electricity, cable TV and internet service, telephone services, trash removal, homeowners association fees, gasoline, food, personal care such as hairstyling, healthcare and medications, entertainment, dining out, and travel. Don't leave anything out! If you're unsure of how much you spend on food, for instance, keep all of your grocery receipts for a week or even a month and add them up. Again, figure a yearly and monthly total. Expense tracking can be a real eye opener and a great incentive to set a budget and live by it.

Now subtract your expenses from your income. The amount you have left over is for paying off debt, putting into an emergency fund, and investing.

Your second pair of numbers is your assets vs. liabilities:

- **Assets.** On this worksheet, list all property and cash you own that has significant value. First, make a realistic assessment of the value of your home by estimating what it would sell for if you sold it today. Add in your savings, CDs, and any stocks you currently own. If you own collectibles and other property that appreciate in value, estimate what they're worth and add them to the total. Your vehicles can be considered an asset, but keep in mind that nearly all vehicles depreciate with every passing year.

- **Liabilities.** This worksheet is for listing money you owe. Start with the total amount left for you to pay on all of your mortgages and home equity loans. Add the total amount of your car loans, student loans, medical debt, revolving credit card debt, private debt such as loans from family members, and any other money you're legally obligated to pay back at some point.

Subtract your liabilities from your assets. The result is your net worth. If this figure has a minus sign in front of it because your liabilities are higher than your assets, then you have what's known as a negative net worth. Although this isn't the best position to be in, it's not so unusual if you're young and just starting out building your assets. Over time, you can turn the negative into a positive.

There's one more number you need to know if you're in the habit of borrowing money, and that's your *debt to income ratio* (DTI). Banks and other lenders look at this figure as closely as they look at your credit score when you apply for a loan. DTI is usually calculated as a monthly percentage of your *gross income*, which is your income before taxes. Go back to your expenses worksheet and add up all of your monthly debt payments, such as the mortgage bill, home equity loan payment, car payment, and monthly credit card bills. You will also need your current gross monthly income before taxes. The DTI formula is calculated with this formula:

monthly expenses / gross monthly income

Convert the decimal figure to a percentage by multiplying it times 100 and adding a % symbol. For example, if your monthly debt payments are $2,500 per month and your gross monthly income is $4,500 per month, your DTI is 56 percent, which isn't good. Twenty-five percent is considered a good, safe DTI, and if you're above 36 percent, lenders will charge you extra interest as a high-risk borrower, or not lend to you at all. If you have a high DTI, consider whether paying down debt might be a better use of your disposable income than investing in the stock market.

Finally, take a look at yourself – your investment knowledge, and your personality. What is your level of familiarity with the investment world? Do you know what fundamental analysis is and how to conduct one? (See Chapter 5.) Do you know the definitions of investment terminology such as diversification and asset allocation (see Chapter 5), fixed-income products (see Chapter 1), and dividends (see Chapters 8 and 9)?

If you don't know the answers yet, don't worry. That's where personality comes into play. Do you love learning new skills? Are you independent by nature and able to teach yourself? Are you comfortable using the internet to look up information? Do you enjoy working with numbers? Maybe the most important question of all is whether the idea of investing truly excites you. Can you picture yourself waking up in the morning and looking forward to checking on your stocks or researching a promising lead in a new market?

If you have answered no to the majority of these questions, then you don't need to cut yourself off from the investment world altogether. Many people (probably most people) are like you and prefer to let someone else manage their investments for them. You can still get great value out of learning the information in this book if you decide to put your money into a managed fund and let someone else build your portfolio. It's always best to understand at least the basic concepts of where your money is going, even if you don't have direct, hands-on responsibility for investing it.

If you answered yes to most of these questions, then buckle up – your adventure is just beginning!

Investing vs. Paying Off Debt

One of the most common questions asked by the would-be investor is whether it's better to use one's disposable income for investment, or for paying off debt. The strongest argument for choosing investment even if you have some debt is that the annual return from equity investments is higher than the interest rate on some loans. For example, the Standard & Poor's 500 (see Chapter 4, How Stocks Are Traded) has recently returned an annual average of about 9.6 percent, and dividend stocks can perform even better. Interest rates on student loan debt average between 3 and 7 percent, while home equity loans are available for well under 5 percent APR, and some car loans are available at 0 percent interest. If you have a high tolerance for risk, it does make sense from a numbers perspective to simply make your monthly payments on your debt, make sure you have an easily accessible fund for emergencies, and put anything left over into the stock market.

The strongest argument in favor of getting out of debt before you start to invest is the risk of carrying debt. Many loans have variable interest rates, which exposes you to the whims of the market, or worse, the whims of politicians, especially in the case of student loans. You simply don't know whether Congress will decide to double the interest rate on your federal student loans (as it did in 2013), or if the chairman of the Federal Reserve will decide to loosen up the ceiling on interest rates to stimulate the economy after nearly a decade of tight control designed to hold down inflation. Another variable is that the stock market has no guarantees, while if you pay down your debt, you can be certain that you will never owe that money again. A third variable is uncertainty in the job market, which has become a fact of life after 2007. As long as you have income, servicing your debt is easy enough, but if you get laid off or downsized, being debt free will buy you time and peace of mind while you're finding another job. Think hard about it. Personal bankruptcy filings have increased exponentially in recent years, and people who formerly had six-figure incomes are among them. I don't want to scare you, but takes a long time to come back from a Chapter 7 or 13.

Investing vs. Saving

I view stock investing as a minimum 10 year commitment, and 20 years is even better. The market fluctuates in the short term in ways that are impossible to predict with certainty. Sure, any number of financial gurus will offer you a formula to "beat the market" (usually for a price), but a few weeks of following their advice on a financial simulation website will open your eyes (see Chapter 7, Time to Invest). It sure opened mine.

Between 2008 and 2012, the US stock market experienced a downturn (called a "bear market") followed by a long period of stagnation, where the average stock price hardly went up at all. The US Treasury has taken some extreme measures to hold down inflation to protect consumers and the stock market. These anti-inflation measures have kept prices on consumer goods from spiraling out of control, and have prevented the stagnant stock market from losing ground to inflation. A stagnant market means that most investors don't lose money, but they don't make money either. It's true that individual stocks may perform better than the market average, but guessing which ones is a high-stakes challenge.

So if you're looking to make a profit on your investments in less than 10 years to reach a particular financial goal, such as buying a home, or saving for a college education that's less than 10 years away, or getting out of debt, the stock market isn't the place for you. Choose an investment with low risk and the highest return you can get. A savings account is the safest place for emergency money that you might need in a hurry, while a money market savings account offers a decent return with low risk and acceptable liquidity.

Interest-Bearing Accounts

- **Savings Accounts:** these venerable interest-bearing

accounts are offered by banks at an interest rate that has barely kept pace with inflation in the past decade. Their FDIC guarantee is a plus, and of course they're as liquid as an investment can get. You simply write a withdrawal slip.

- **Small Savers Certificates:** These are a special type of savings account with a minimum opening deposit amount (usually $500, but can be as low as $100) and a fixed maturity term, normally 12 months, during which you can't withdraw your money. Their interest rates tend to be a bit higher than conventional savings accounts, and they enjoy FDIC protection. Some banks allow you to add funds to your SSC before the maturity period ends.

- **Certificates of Deposit (CDs):** banks heavily advertise these fixed-value, interest-bearing notes as a better alternative than savings account, but the interest rate is typically below 5 percent. With their minimum commitment requirement of several months, CDs aren't liquid. Like savings accounts, they do carry FDIC insurance against loss.

- **Money Market Savings Accounts:** Many banks offer savings accounts with interest rates based on the money market, which are typically higher than conventional savings accounts. These accounts are FDIC-insured and have a minimum deposit requirement – $1,000 or sometimes higher, into the five figures. These accounts allow you to draw checks on the account, but there are restrictions on the number of them you can write per month, and some require you to maintain a minimum balance.

Be sure to learn the difference between a money market savings account (sometimes called a money market account or MMA), which is offered by a bank and is FDIC-insured, and a money market fund (MMF). MMFs are investment vehicles offered by mutual funds, brokers, and sometimes banks. These funds invest in the money market, which consists of short-term securities that always have a share price of $1. You only earn money on them when their interest rate (referred to as "yield") goes up, because their share price stays consistent. They are not FDIC-insured, and because they fluctuate like any other security, investing in them involves risk. The confusing part is that banks can offer both MMAs and MMFs, so be sure to ask which product you're getting, and whether it's covered by the FDIC.

Retirement Planning

If you are still in your employment years, your number one investment priority needs to be participating in a retirement plan. Even if you are under 35, don't neglect this important part of managing your money. Unless you are already retired, your retirement plan from your job is probably a "defined contribution plan." Your company deducts a portion of your paycheck each pay period and places it in an investment account. Many employers offer matching funds for employee pensions, and it goes without saying that you should take full advantage of this if it's available. Large employers will often give a 2-to-1 match – that is, for every $1 you allow them to withhold from your paycheck and deposit in your IRA or other tax-deferred annuity fund, your company will deposit $2. No matter how young you are, or how hard it is for you to imagine being retired, always take advantage of a fund match. Turning it down is like turning down free money.

Retirement accounts go by different names, including 401k, IRA, Keough, SEP, and others, all with slightly different regulations. What they all have in common is that they're tax-deferred. You deposit money in them tax free while you're working, and don't withdraw it until the required retirement age. At that time, since you're no longer working, you'll be in a lower tax bracket and won't pay as high a tax on the withdrawal.

Most tax-deferred retirement accounts are invested in mutual funds. Although "cafeteria" benefit plans may offer you some choice in the type of mutual fund you prefer, such as which sector (see Chapter 3), or short-term vs. long-term return stocks, the reality is you don't have much say in where the money goes. I made a point of forming a relationship with the outside provider that administered my company's retirement fund, and I asked a lot of questions so I could exercise maximum control over my benefits. I'm glad I did.

Budgeting for Investment

If you feel that your financial situation is stable enough to start investing in stocks, then one way to test the waters is to arrange for a certain sum from each paycheck to be deposited in your brokerage account. You can then set up a plan with your broker for investing those funds. If you don't make enough money with each paycheck to justify the brokerage fees of making a new trade every week, then your broker can hold your funds in your brokerage account until they accumulate to a certain threshold, at which time your broker will invest them according to your plan.

I'm personally familiar with the another purpose of automatic investment plans. When I first started investing, my wife and I held large amounts of money in safe, low-return accounts such as savings and CDs. Nedra was more cautious than me about the stock market, so we agreed to set up a plan that would slowly dribble in money from our CD account over the next year, while leaving more than half of that balance untouched. That gave us a partially passive investment plan, leaving me free to focus on the more enjoyable, profitable aspects of investing while gaining some experience in the market a little at a time.

Chapter 3
How Stocks Make Money

My initial understanding of the market was that a stock somehow made money for me when it went up in value. I didn't really understand exactly how this happened, though, until I started investing. I wish I had understood it earlier. While I would have continued to invest in growth stocks, I also would have bought stocks that paid dividends far sooner than I ended up doing. If you don't understand why these terms are important, read on to learn how stocks make money for investors.

Why a Company Issues Stock

Why would a company decide to become publicly traded by selling shares of its stock on the open market? Why not just limit ownership in the company to a few wealthy investors and keep complete control over its operations and the makeup of its board of directors?

The answer is that 100 percent private ownership is a viable option, and many successful companies never go public. To own a piece of these companies, you would need millions of dollars and the business connections that go with that income level.

The reason companies give up the control of private ownership is access to more investment money – way more. If a company wants to raise money for research and development, new products, entry into new markets, financial growth, or acquiring competitors, there's nothing like issuing shares of stock and selling them to the public to raise cash in the hundreds of millions.

An additional advantage for companies who issue stock is the low cost of using it to obtain capital. Loans, bonds, and other debt securities (see Chapter 1) have to be paid back, with interest. Selling stock is like an interest-free loan for a company. Sure, there's the overhead cost of managing the shares through an investment bank, but nonetheless, the stock market provides a ready-made vehicle for a company to go out and get additional funds when it wants to grow.

Kinds of Stock

There are many different ways to classify stocks into categories. The most common ways are by sector, and by market cap.

Sector Investing

Some investors only buy stocks in one industry, called a sector. For example, you might only invest in technology companies, or pharmaceutical companies. The logic behind sector investing is that it's easier to evaluate the opportunities and risks of a stock if you know how other stocks in the same sector behave. There are even special indexes (lists of stocks) that track all of the stocks in one particular sector. These indexes usually have exchange traded funds (ETFs – see Chapter 4) with their own ticker symbols, making it easy to invest in a particular sector that you've studied and gained some knowledge of.

I like tracking sector exchange traded funds (ETFs – see below and Chapter 4), even if I don't buy shares in them. They're such an efficient way to track how the various sectors of the economy are doing. When a big, general index like the S&P 500 is doing well, that doesn't necessarily mean that the overall market is doing well. Most of the time, a couple of sectors are turning in a strong performance and making the rest of the index look better than it really is. I track sector ETFs to see which ones are thriving and which ones to avoid. I even examine the strongest performers within each sector and only buy those stocks if the rest are doing poorly.

Here is a list of the major sectors:

- **Consumer discretionary:** companies that make non-necessary goods, including retail, media, hotels, luxury items, cars, leisure and clothing

- **Consumer staples:** companies that make things people will buy no matter what, including food, beverages, personal items, and cigarettes

- **Energy:** fuel production companies, including oil and gas, renewables, and the products, equipment and services that support these industries

- **Financial services:** all financial companies, including insurance, banking, capital markets, trusts, credit cards and loans, and real estate (real estate is sometimes classified in its own sector)

- **Healthcare:** hospitals, doctors, medical equipment, pharmaceuticals, biotech, and health and science research equipment and services

- **Industrial:** anything related to manufacturing and shipping material goods, including aerospace, machinery, railroads, construction, engineering, airlines and logistics

- **Materials:** producers and extractors of raw materials for manufacturing, companies that extract or produce the raw materials, including chemicals, mining, forest products, packaging and construction materials

- **Technology:** computers, software, hardware, telecommunications services and equipment, semiconductors, IT and wireless services, internet, and office electronics. (Telecommunications is sometimes classified in its own sector.)

- **Utilities:** companies involved in electrical and gas utilities, as well as power producers and energy traders

Market Cap Investing

Another way to classify stocks is by company size. Investors use a formula called market capitalization (market cap for short) to determine size. The formula is:

Current price of a single share X number of shares available on the market

For example, a company whose stock price is $200 per share and has issued 30 million shares would have a market cap of $6 billion.

Companies can be classified according to their market cap. The cutoff figures vary, but the rule of thumb is:

- $50 million or less: nano cap
- $50 million to $300 million: small cap
- $300 million to $2 billion: small cap
- $2 to $10 billion: mid cap
- $10 billion or more: large cap (also called "blue chip" stocks)

I like the Russell Indexes for tracking companies according to their capitalization. Check out the Russell 2000 for a list of small-cap stocks in the US.

Some investors only buy stocks at one capitalization level, usually large cap. There's a persistent belief in the financial press and among some investors and financial advisors that a big company means small risk. If you think back a bit, though, and recall the internal fraud that took down Worldcom and Enron, or the changing market conditions that led to the General Motors bankruptcy, you'll realize that size isn't bulletproof protection from losing money in the stock market.

The other thing to remember is that phrases like "small cap" and "big cap" are relative terms. The market today is much larger and is dominated by a list of big players that dwarf smaller companies in their sheer size and share of available investment capital. The fact that these giants are so large does not necessarily mean that small-cap companies are undercapitalized. Many of these companies have no desire to compete with the likes of Wal-Mart and McDonalds, preferring to excel in a niche market that's too small for the big players to bother with. For example, a smaller mid-cap company like Gulfport Energy, with $4 billion in capitalization, would have been considered a large cap company 30 or 40 years ago.

There's one type of stock where I do follow the advice of the financial press, and that's penny stocks. Some (but not all) nano-cap stocks are penny stocks, and although the idea of stumbling onto a bargain for pennies per share and watching it grow into an empire is appealing, the way these stocks are sold is just too risky. For one thing, the SEC disclosure rules for penny stocks are less strict than for larger companies, so there's just not enough transparency to reassure me. Often times, penny stocks are issued as an IPO because an insolvent company wants to dump its liabilities onto unsuspecting shareholders. Penny stock brokers are complicit in the scheme, and if you buy even one of these duds, they'll hound you at all hours of the day and night trying to get you to buy more. These people have a reputation as sharks for a reason.

Capital Appreciation

The first way stocks make money is the best known. You buy a stock at a certain price, and just as you hoped, the value of that stock increases. This is called "growth investing," because you earn money if the share price grows.

OK, so now the stock you bought for $10 per share is worth $11 per share, and you pocket the difference. Wait, not so fast. Although your portfolio is now worth more on paper, you don't actually make the money until you sell the stock. If you do sell the stock, the $1 difference is income for you (minus any brokerage fees for the sale, of course). You pay taxes on that income, but it's taxed at the capital gain rate, which is about half of what you pay on your salary as an employee.

If you're following a long-term investment strategy, or you want to avoid paying excessive brokerage fees and capital gains taxes for frequent buying and selling of stocks, then growth investing means accepting long periods of time where you might be wealthy, but only on paper.

Dividends

Dividends are a lesser-known way that stocks make money, but more people are becoming interested (see Chapters 8 and 9). In periods of low growth like the period of 2008-2012, investing in companies that pay dividends becomes more attractive. A dividend is an agreement with a company whose stock you own to pay you a portion of its profits at a certain interval, usually quarterly. Not all companies pay dividends. Those that do tend to be older, more stable companies whose stock prices don't fluctuate as much as newer, smaller companies. Growth investors look for low prices on these companies' stocks, while those who invest for income see buying stock in these companies as simply the cost of entry for receiving their dividend payout. These two approaches aren't mutually exclusive.

If you sell the stock in a company that pays dividends, you probably won't make a huge profit. But why would you sell if you're getting a cash payout every quarter? Dividend investing means you're actually getting paid to own the stock, not just when you sell. That's why dividend investment is called "investing for income."

Compounding

Compounding is a third way that your stock investments make money for you. To realize the benefit of compounding, you take the profit from your initial investment and add it to that investment, instead of cashing it out and spending it. Now you're earning interest, capital gains, or dividends on a larger chunk of money. When you profit from this sum, you roll the profits back in and make your investment even larger. Over time, your profit grows to an amount far higher than what you would have made from your initial investment alone.

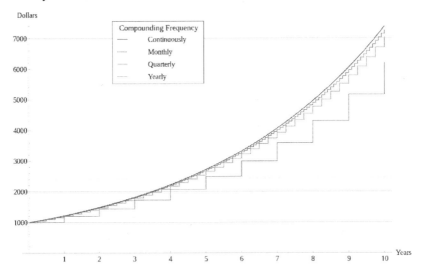

Dollars

Compounding Frequency
——— Continuously
······· Monthly
········ Quarterly
········ Yearly

The power of compounding over time (image by Jetson25)

If your investment portfolio includes stock in companies that pay dividends, then compounding is your secret weapon. Dividend investing goes hand in hand with compounding, thanks to special reinvestment plans aimed at dividend investors, called dividend reinvestment plans (DRIPs – see Chapter 9). A DRIP allows you to buy a single share, or even a fraction of a share, of a dividend-paying company, receive whatever dividend amount you're entitled to, and reinvest it in the company. Best of all, DRIPs don't require you to pay a brokerage fee.

DRIPs reinvest your dividends for you, so you're continually feeding your profit into an ever-higher investment and earning more dividends every quarter. This is truly investing for income.

Initial Public Offerings

When a company issues stock for the first time, this is called an initial public offering, or IPO. The IPO is the signal event that a company has gone from private to public ownership.

IPOs can raise hundreds of millions of dollars for a company looking for cash to expand its operations. Some companies go public almost immediately, while others, such as Facebook and Google, hold out for years in private ownership before finally going public.

How does this affect the retail investor? Usually, not at all. Unless you have hundreds of thousands of dollars to invest, or are exceptionally well connected, IPO stock will be bought up before small investors get a chance at it. If you have your heart set on an IPO, you will have to wait for it to reach the secondary market, where the investors who bought it at the IPO start trading it openly.

Bull vs. Bear Markets

You have probably heard of bull and bear markets and wondered why investors talk so much about them. Here are the snapshot definitions.

- In a bull market, stock prices are rising, and investors expect them to keep rising. This means stocks are in demand and there is more willingness to take risks. Bull markets signal a prosperous economy.

- In a bear market, stock prices are falling, and investors expect them to keep falling. When stock prices fall, investors lose money, so there's less demand for stocks and less willingness to take risks. Bear markets are a sign of a weak economy.

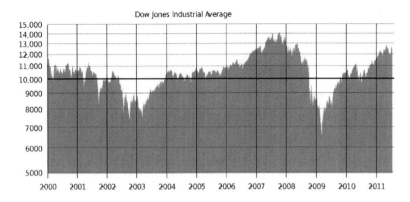

Chart of the Dow Jones Industrial Average from 2000-2010 showing the bear markets of 2000-2002 and 2007-2009

Deep in the financial district in New York City, there's a 7,100-pound bronze sculpture of a bull. Its huge horns and fierce expression embody the spirit of Wall Street, ready to charge forward and embrace prosperity. I've always found it a bit humorous that there's no sculpture of a bear next to the bull. Nobody likes bear markets, but stock prices can't rise forever, so they are a fact of life.

Like some investors, I believe that bear markets are great investment opportunities. Here's why: bear market stock prices are low. The fear among growth investors is that in a bear market, stock prices will just keep going down and they'll lose money even if they buy at rock bottom prices. I invest for income as well as for growth, which partially insulates me from bear markets. I want to buy stocks at the lowest possible price and collect the dividends while waiting for an upturn in the market, so the bear is my friend.

Spotlight: General Motors: Then and Now

In the early days of the auto industry, American cars were king. Following World War II, the incredible growth of the "Big Three" automakers (General Motors, Ford, and Chrysler) drove the fast-growing economy, supported the birth of the Baby Boomer generation, and made Detroit the fourth largest city in the US between 1920 and 1950. The American auto industry created hundreds of thousands of jobs directly, and millions of spin-off jobs with suppliers. This resulted in a thriving middle class that spent billions of dollars in discretionary income and powered the US economy into world domination. The saying, "As GM goes, so goes the nation," became part of conventional wisdom.

Unfortunately, that saying was just as true in the bad times as well as the good. General Motors was so prosperous that it became complacent. When the first Japanese economy cars hit the US market in the late 1970s, GM's research and development department snapped up a fleet of them and tore them down to parts at its gated proving grounds in Milford, Michigan. The engineers in their blue coats tsk-tsked and made fun of the "econoboxes," as they came to be called. "These will never sell," they scoffed. "Americans like big, fast cars."

True, that. But the mid-1970s saw the first energy crisis hit the country due to the 1973 oil embargo by the OPEC cartel in the Middle East and the 1975 hostage crisis. Gas lines were long, and prices tripled within a year. The new squeeze on the economy meant that big, expensive cars that gulped fuel weren't an instant sell anymore. More and more Americans were growing curious about those little foreign cars that sipped gas and didn't have to be replaced when they hit 75,000 miles. Of course, Japanese cars did have a huge problem that didn't become apparent right away: rust. Their steel was of such poor quality that after a few Midwestern winters they turned into a mass of holes. But by the mid-1980s that problem was well on its way to being resolved. Meanwhile, GM was scrambling to catch up by releasing its Chevette model, but it was too little, too late.

By 2005, the foreign invasion had taken its toll on GM. It cut 30,000 jobs and closed five assembly plants, and losses that year for the automotive giant totaled a staggering $8.6 billion. For years, GM stock had paid a dividend of 50 cents per share, but at the end of 2005, it took the unprecedented step of reducing that amount by half – a move that did not inspire investor confidence, given all the other bad news that appeared that year. At its peak, it employed 600,000 Americans, owned 46 percent of the American auto market, and was the Fortune One company – the largest in the world. By 2005, its market share had fallen to 26 percent. Robotics and other efficiencies in car production slashed manufacturing jobs even further.

At the end of 2008, GM was $3.9 billion in debt and failed to pay dividends. In early 2009 it decided to file for bankruptcy. Even though it was no secret that GM had been foundering for years, the Chapter 11 filing sent shock waves throughout the world economy. Hundreds of thousands of jobs were lost as suppliers that GM owed money to were put on the list of creditors, and received pennies on the dollar. Shares of GM stock became virtually worthless.

For a time it seemed that the company would dissolve. $49.5 billion was needed to keep it afloat, and no lender could be found that was willing to risk that sum on a company that had been losing money for years. In the end, it was the United States treasury that stepped forward with the money and assumed a 61 percent stake in the company. The move was politically controversial and was used as ammunition by both conservatives and liberals in the national debate about the role of government in the economy. Several smaller automakers that GM had swallowed up in mergers, like Volvo and Saab, were sold off, and the company offloaded its Hummer brand to China at a bargain basement price.

In the end, the automotive giant proved impossible to kill. New stock was issued and wary investors slowly gained confidence in the "new GM." The government sold its last remaining shares of GM in 2013, and the company sold 9.7 million vehicles worldwide, 4 percent more than in 2012. China proved to be a major customer, with sales of GM vehicles increasing by 11 percent. In a ground-breaking decision, the company appointed Mary Barra as CEO, the first time in history that a US car company has ever hired a woman to run the show.

In January 2014, General Motors announced to much fanfare that it would pay a quarterly dividend of 30 cents per share on its common stock in March. The announcement sent its share price soaring by 3 percent, and sent a message to the world that an investment in GM was again one that could be made with confidence.

Chapter 4
How Stocks Are Traded

People talk about the "stock market," but not everyone knows how it works. Before I retired and started investing, my mental picture of the stock market came from the movies and television shows, with tense-looking traders barking buy and sell orders on the floor of the New York Stock Exchange. As you'll see, this picture is only partly true. Although the physical NYSE still exists, more and more trading is being done electronically. That's good news for retail investors because it makes more and better trading strategies available, accompanied by lower fees.

How Stocks Are Valued

Companies have a wide array of choices when they initially structure their stock price before going public. The rule of thumb is, the more shares issued, the lower the price per share. For example, a company that wants to raise $200 million could issue 10 million shares at $20 per share. It could also issue 20 million shares at $10 per share, or 40 million shares at $5 per share. Any of these strategies would raise $200 million if all shares were sold.

This rule can help you understand that the price of a stock isn't really that important for determining its value. The only thing a higher stock price really means is that you're buying fewer shares for the same amount of money. If you want a useful estimate of a stock's value, you need to understand its price-to-earnings ratio. The formula for calculating the PE ratio is:

Price per share / earnings per share in the past year

The result of this formula, the PE ratio, is a useful tool for comparing the values of not only individual stocks, but mutual funds, exchange-traded funds, and even entire indexes.

There's no magic number for the PE ratio that makes a stock a good buy, because there are so many other factors that go into the decision to purchase. Is the company growing or shrinking? How many of the past five years did it make a profit? How fast has its stock price appreciated? Does it pay dividends? But you can tuck the number 15 into your back pocket, because that's the average PE ratio of stocks in the US.

Stock Exchanges

A stock exchange is a location where shares of stock are traded. Historically, stock exchanges were physical locations. The New York Stock Exchange was the first stock exchange in the United States, and it still has a physical location on Wall Street in Lower Manhattan.

Today, electronic stock exchanges are pushing physical stock exchanges out of the way. The NASDAQ was founded in 1971 by the National Association of Security Dealers as an all-electronic exchange. The NASDAQ is sometimes called an over-the-counter (OTC) exchange, since there are no middlemen on the floor. The New York Stock Exchange is slowly converting to electronic trading, but in keeping with tradition since the early 1800s, the NYSE still posts its trades on signage (although the traditional chalkboard has been abandoned in favor of electronic monitors) and traders call out their trades on the floor.

Most of the world's major economic powers have their own stock exchanges. After the NYSE and the NASDAQ, which are the world's largest and next-largest, respectively, the top ten are London, Tokyo, Hong Kong, Shanghai, Canada's TMX Group,

Germany's Deutsche Börse, Australia, and Bombay.

The Major Indexes

An index is a survey of the stock market. An index company, such as the Dow Jones Industrial Average, picks a limited number of stocks that it believes represent the performance of the entire market, or a sector within the market, and averages their performance to arrive at a number that investors can use to gauge the performance of the market, or compare it with individual stocks or managed funds. The US has three major indexes – Dow Jones Industrial Average, the Standard & Poor's 500, and the Nasdaq Composite – and a number of minor ones. Each index has its own stock chart with opening and closing value, volume, and average volume, just like individual company stocks.

As you start to watch the different indexes, you will realize that they seldom move in parallel, unless there's an earth-shattering event like a major move upward, or a catastrophic crash. I use the indexes to track and compare different sectors and varying levels of market capitalization (see Chapter 3), so I can zero in on the ones that offer the most benefit to me according to my personal investment approach. I also use them to track my investments in exchange-traded funds (ETFs – see below).

Here is a list of some of the better-known indexes:

Dow Jones Industrial Average (DJIA)

The Dow is the first index in the US, dating back to 1896. It tracks the stocks of the top 30 largest companies in the world that are traded on the New York Stock Exchange and the NASDAQ and averages their price according to a complex price-weighting formula. The DJIA encompasses approximately 25 percent of the US market. All of the Dow companies are large and well established, and all of them pay out dividends (see Chapters 8 and 9). Because the US financial media favors reporting on blue-chip stocks, when investors talk about "the market," they're usually talking about the status of the DJIA. There's nothing wrong with this if it matches your investment preferences, but if you're looking at mid-cap or small-cap stocks, or if your investments are heavily weighted toward technology or other non-industrial companies, you're probably better off looking at an index with a larger sample size such as the S&P 500.

Along with its famous industrial index, the Dow has two specialty indexes and a composite index, all of which use the same price-weighting formula. The Dow Jones Transportation Average (DJTA) surveys the top 20 US transportation stocks and predates even the DJIA, dating back to the days when railroads were king. If you subscribe to the "Dow Theory," you'll watch the DJTA and compare it with the DJIA. If the DJIA stays up but the DJTA falls, that could mean that goods are being manufactured but are not actually being shipped to their destinations due to weak demand. Similarly, the Dow Jones Utility Average (DJUA) price weights the largest 15 US utility stocks. According to the Dow Theory, this index is a harbinger of rising interest rates, since utilities routinely borrow large amounts of money. Finally, the Dow Jones 65 Composite Average is a price-weighted composite of the DJIA, the DJTA, and the DJUA, totaling 65 stocks in all. Although this composite gives the Dow more breadth and depth, it's still a bit skimpy on service and information economy industries such as finance, technology, and health care.

What sets the Dow apart from other indexes is its price-weighted indexing formula, which adds up the price per share of each company and divides the sum by the number of companies in the index. Because the average gives the same weight to each company's share price regardless of its market cap, it's heavily influenced by stocks with the highest share price. In contrast, the other indexes use a market-weighted formula, which adds market capitalization into the equation, thus equalizing share prices. Not only is this a more accurate indicator of the market, but it makes comparisons between different indexes easier.

Standard and Poor's 500

This is the other go-to index for US investors. It evaluates the top 500 publicly-traded companies on the New York Stock Exchange or the NASDAQ and encompasses about 70 percent of the US market's total value. The S&P is far larger and more diverse than the Dow. It takes in many sectors, such as consumer staples, health care, industrials, energy, and financials, which makes it the most comprehensive index of the US market. The investor who uses the S&P 500 as the measuring stick for how the market is doing tends to be focused on stocks from diverse sectors and market cap levels. To make things a bit more interesting, the DJIA and the S&P have both been owned by mega-publisher McGraw Hill Financial since 2012, although they are managed and marketed as separate entities.

NASDAQ Composite Index

The NASDAQ index is a compilation of the world's top 5,000 companies that are traded on the NASDAQ exchange. Like the NASDAQ exchange itself, this index is heavily weighted toward technology stocks, along with service-based industries such as finance. If you're interested in small-cap stocks and all the higher risks and potential rewards that go with them, you're most likely to find them on the NASDAQ.

Wilshire 5,000 Total Market Index

This is an index of the top 6,700 companies based in the US and traded on a US exchange (the 5,000 was its original figure, but it has grown since then). More diverse than all of the other indexes, its relative newness to the industry (it was established in 1974) makes it less used than older, more established indexes.

Russell Indexes

The Russells are an index family covering the top companies in the US. These indexes are segmented according to their market cap (see Chapter 3), making them extremely useful for investors who prefer to make their picks according to this metric. Its two best-known indexes are the Russell 3000, which tracks the 3,000 largest US companies based in their market capitalization; and the Russell 2000, which tracks the 2,000 smallest companies on the Russell 3000. Investors who favor small-cap stocks also tend to favor the Russell Indexes.

Passive vs. Active Investing

I've found it helpful to think of passive vs. active investing as a continuum, rather than as black and white categories. At the extremely passive end, we have everyone's proverbial grandmother faithfully putting her money into a bank savings account, where she knows it will be safe and (we hope) will earn enough interest to keep pace with inflation. At the extremely active end we have the day trader, who buys stock online and sells it five minutes later when the share price goes up a few dollars. There are many legitimate investment strategies between these two extremes.

By far the most mainstream investment strategy is "buy and hold." This approach is initially active because the investor makes decisions on which stocks to purchase, but once the investment is made, it becomes passive. You simply weather the ups and downs in the market and hang on to the stock no matter what until you decide to cash out. Growth investors (see Chapter 5) assume that the long-term trend of the market is always up, regardless of short-term adjustments, while dividend investors hold a stock regardless of its share price, unless it stops paying dividends. Both types of investors are practicing a buy and hold strategy.

Stocks vs. Managed Funds

My early stock trades were all individuals stocks. For example, I'd contact my broker and tell him I wanted to buy 10 shares of PepsiCo, and those shares would be added to my portfolio. I didn't start learning about managed funds and ETFs until I had been investing for almost a year. Although funds aren't always the best choice for the retail investor, I wish I had learned about them earlier so I could make an informed choice, especially in the area of portfolio diversification.

Individual Stocks

All publicly traded stocks are offered on the market as individual shares. You don't have to buy several companies' stocks in one bundle as you would with a fund. Buying individual stocks has the advantage of simplicity. You know how each stock you own is performing, since it's not rolled into a fund. Accumulating money is simple as well – all income from selling your shares ends up in the same place, your brokerage account, where you can use it to purchase other stocks.

The disadvantage of individual stock trading is that diversification takes so much effort. You would have to spend days or weeks evaluating individual stocks to match the diversity of a fund. Diversity is important because it means that if one stock in your portfolio goes down, the others absorb the hit by staying steady or going up. When you're only invested in a few stocks, your investment money is vulnerable.

Mutual Funds

A mutual fund is a pool of money from many different investors that the fund manager uses to buy a portfolio of stocks for them. Most mutual funds are actively managed, meaning the fund manager makes judgment calls about which stocks to purchase for the fund's investors. Index funds (see below) are passively managed, meaning that the fund simply duplicates whatever stocks are included in that particular index.

To invest in a mutual fund, you simply contact a financial management firm that offers them, make the required minimum investment (usually in the four figures), and let the fund manager do the rest, so it's a passive investment for you. Most tax-deferred retirement accounts (see Chapter 2), such as IRAs and 401k's, are invested in mutual funds. Money market funds are a special type of mutual fund that invests in short-term money market securities. Unlike money market savings accounts (see

Chapter 2), these funds are not FDIC-insured, and for all practical purposes they should be treated like any other mutual fund investment.

Mutual funds have some advantages, the biggest being diversification. It's hard to beat the diversity of an actively managed fund, which means it takes a pretty devastating downtown in the entire market to make a mutual fund lose money over the long term. Many retail investors like the hands-off aspect of letting a fund manager handle their investments for them.

Fees are a substantial down side of investing in mutual funds. Fund managers don't work for free, and any money you pay them as service fees is money you don't have left to invest. Inquire closely about service fees before you decide to invest in an actively managed fund.

A second disadvantage of mutual funds is that the fund manager, not you, votes the fund's shares, since the fund owns those shares. The law requires the fund to disclose its voting record to the general public by filing an annual form with the SEC.

A third disadvantage is the stock portfolio of a mutual fund is private information known only to the fund manager. You will know the general characteristics of the fund's individual stocks (usually described by sector or market cap), but not the stocks themselves.

Index Funds

Unlike mutual funds, the individual stock makeup of the indexes is public information. Many financial managers use this information to build products called "index funds" which duplicate the stocks listed in a particular index, complete with the exact number of shares allocated to each company. Index funds are considered passively managed funds because no human judgment is involved – the fund simply duplicates the index and makes that portfolio available to investors.

One advantage of index funds is that you know exactly where

your money is invested and can use the index portfolio as a diversification tool. Another advantage is their performance, which traditionally has matched or slightly exceeded actively managed funds such as mutual funds. Yet another advantage is the lack of brokerage fees. Because the indexes seldom change their makeup, the fund doesn't change its makeup either, saving you the costs of adding and deleting stocks.

Index funds are available through mutual fund brokerages, such as Vanguard, and as exchange-traded funds (ETFs).

ETFs

An exchange-traded fund is a publicly-traded company that offers its investors shares in an index fund. To invest in an ETF, you simply buy shares of the ETF company's stock, and the value of your shares in the ETF rises or falls as the index falls.

Exchange-traded funds are considered by many investors to be the best of both worlds. You buy their stock just as you would buy an individual stock, through a brokerage account, but you get the diversity of a mutual fund. You also get transparency, since the stock makeup of the indexes is publicly available information. And because they are managed electronically, they tend to have lower overheads. As a shareholder in the ETF company, you can vote by proxy on its management and other shareholder decisions.

Like any other equity investment, the advantages of ETFs are not an excuse to stop monitoring your investments. Pay close attention to brokerage fees, and ask your broker questions about the particular index that an ETF tracks. A few ETFs have started tracking obscure "boutique indexes" that change their makeup frequently, allowing them to rake in more brokerage fees. I avoid these and stick with ETFs that track established indexes, so I keep my fees low.

SPOTLIGHT: GETTING ACQUAINTED WITH SPIDERS (SPDR ETFs)

The advantages of exchange traded funds (ETFs) are well known. They offer the retail investor the diversity and ease of management of a mutual fund. However, unlike mutual funds, they are passively managed, so their brokerage fee savings are considerable. Those of us who prefer to take charge of our investments are more comfortable relying on an ETF's transparency and our own due diligence, than on a well-paid mutual fund manager whose reputation for investment savvy may or may not be deserved.

If you're interested in ETFs, then you might find "spiders" worth a look. The acronym SPDR stands for Standard & Poor's depository receipt. These ETFs track the S&P 500 index, trading at between around 10 percent of its value. They are bought and sold through a broker, like an individual stock, and have their own ticker symbols.

Spiders are a type of Unit Investment Trust (UIT), meaning that they have a fixed number of shares which are bought and sold on the New York Stock Exchange. Because they sell at a lower price than shares of the full S&P 500 index fund, they offer investors an investment vehicle to own stocks listed in this large index at an affordable price.

UITs have a defined lifespan, after which the asset is returned to the investor, so be aware of the termination date when you buy. When it comes time to vote your shares, you'll be voting a special proxy for the UIT, rather than for the entire index fund.

Spiders have been so successful that they have even been created to track the DJIA. The SPDR Dow Jones Large Cap ETF is a good example. Other SPDRs are cropping up for other indexes, and although they don't yet represent the majority of ETFs, they do take up a sizable portion of this market. Specialty SPDRs that track certain   sectors or market cap levels are becoming more common.

The risks of spiders are the same as all ETFs: because there's no active management, you are at the mercy of the index. When the index goes up, you make money. When it goes down...well, you know the rest. A passively managed investment vehicle does not mean you should manage it passively. If you're not willing to devote a significant amount of your time every week to studying the market and taking note of movements and trends, then you should stick to actively managed funds and delegate the management of your investments to someone who is.

Chapter 5
Learning the Language of Investors

My initial experiences with the stock market were like a visit to a foreign country. The language being spoken contained all kinds of unfamiliar words and phrases that were meaningless to me until I took the responsibility of educating myself. Sure, you can pay someone else to manage your investments, if you're so inclined, and never learn to read a stock chart or a 10-K form. But knowing something about the language of investors gives you so much more control over your money – and you may even find that it's fun.

Investment Resources You Should Read

When I was learning about the stock market, I read everything I could get my hands on, from very basic consumer magazines like *Money*, to the highly technical (and expensive) *AAII Journal*. Now that I have a good background knowledge of the market, I stick to a much smaller list consisting of publications favored by serious retail investors. Some of these are also read by professionals such as bankers and brokers, which means they're top-notch.

- **The Wall Street Journal:** There's no getting around the fact that the WSJ is the number one go-to publication for investors. Its excellent reputation is well deserved. Its only drawback is the sheer volume of information it presents. Here are some shortcuts to help you get the most from your subscription. I start by scanning the front page, zeroing in on the "What's News" section, to see if there's any breaking news that could signal a trend in the market. I then skip to the Marketplace, and then to the Money and Investing sections. It's worth learning how to interpret the market data at the end of the investing section – don't be put off by the fine print. Note that the WSJ is available for e-reader devices. http://online.wsj.com/

- **Investor's Business Daily:** IBD is aimed at serious investors, but it's not just for professionals. The entire magazine is devoted to analysis of the market and individual stocks so you can make your own picks and build your own portfolio. Many of IBD's articles are educational in nature, making it a great resource for the retail investor. IBD is nearly as respected as the WSJ for investment news. Check it out at http://www.investors.com

- **AAII Journal:** Published by the American Association of Individual Investors, this magazine isn't for the beginner, but it's unmatched for advice on picking individual stocks. If you don't want to cash out for this relatively small publication (it's really more of a newsletter), check out their "best of" samples on their website, http://www.aaii.com/journal

The following magazines are aimed more at novice investors, but when I have time I still read them for news that could tip me off to a new trend or growth stock.

- **Kiplinger:** If you're interested in mutual funds, *Kiplinger* is the go-to source. Those who prefer index funds or individual stock picks don't always speak kindly of this magazine, but I think it has a lot of other great things to offer. The articles are easy to read and tackle important topics like saving for retirement, and avoiding unnecessary brokerage fees. They also have a great website with lots of free information: http://www.kiplinger.com/

- **Barron's:** This is another basic-level magazine for the beginning investor, with an emphasis on personal finance and managing your money wisely. It also profiles publicly traded companies and highlights market trends. It's a solid, highly readable publication. http://online.barrons.com

These magazines are more news-oriented than the above publications, but they focus on the economy and business topics.

- **The Economist:** This is an old and respected news magazine that focuses on economics. It does a fantastic job of putting world events into a global context and analyzing the possible consequences. I read it for its international perspective because globalization is a reality that affects the US market, and it's a must-read if you're making foreign investments (see Chapter 10). Their analysis is always intelligent, provocative, and remarkably free of bias. http://www.economist.com/

- **Bloomberg BusinessWeek:** Although it's focused on business and the economy, BusinessWeek is really a news magazine. I like it because it's so comprehensive – it's unusual for them to miss a news story. They're especially good at tracking mergers and acquisitions in the US marketplace, and they cover political events with an eye to the financial side of things. http://www.businessweek.com/

- **Inc.:** Aimed at small businesses, entrepreneurs, and would-be entrepreneurs, *Inc.* can be a good source of news about trends in the business world, particularly involving startups and innovations in the tech sector. http://www.inc.com/

- **Money:** Really more of a personal finance publication than a business magazine, CNN's *Money* magazine has

some good advice for taking charge of your financial picture and saving for retirement.
http://money.cnn.com/magazines/moneymag/

How to Read a Stock Chart

The internet has made it easy to find stock charts for any publicly traded company at any time, for free. The two big search engines, Google and Yahoo, both compile their own branded stock charts and serve them up when you type a company name or ticker symbol into the search box. I prefer to search on Yahoo Finance, http://finance.yahoo.com because the result gives me more information than Google, and the graph is easier to read. Marketwatch, http://www.marketwatch.com is another useful site for tracking companies.

From the top, let's start with the identifying information. You will see the company name, the current date and time, and the stock's ticker symbol, composed of the 2 to 5 capital letters that stand for the company name. Next to the ticker is the exchange that the chart is drawing its data from, such as NYSE. (Marketwatch has a nifty extra feature that allows you to compare the stock performance across more than one exchange if the stock is traded on multiple exchanges.) The current price per share will be prominently displayed. Color coded arrow symbols show whether the stock closed lower or higher at the close of trading than at opening that day.

The price graph should allow you to adjust the time period displayed from one day to all time, with several intervals in between, so you can evaluate its performance in both the short and long term.

Below the price graph, you'll see the volume and average volume, either in a smaller bar graph, or in text display. This tells you how many shares changed hands during the current trading day, and you can also access historical data. Active traders and technical analysts (see below) use spikes in volume as an indicator of a change in a stock's value, either upward or downward, as investors move to acquire more shares, or sell them off.

The Importance of a Diverse Portfolio

Investors disagree vigorously on many things, but you won't hear any of them arguing against diversification. While they may argue about *how* diverse you should be (see Warren Buffett's thoughts in Chapter 6), nobody will tell you to go out and invest in only one stock. The prevailing wisdom is that you need at least 25 to 30 stocks in your portfolio in order to reduce your exposure to risk. The goal is to let the price increases of some of your stocks offset the price decreases of your other stocks during ordinary fluctuations in the market. If you've made good picks, and the economy is fairly healthy, the result should be a net gain over time.

The challenge for the retail investor is finding those 25 to 30 stocks at an affordable price. Blue-chip stocks such as McDonald's and PepsiCo trade in the neighborhood of $85 per share, with General Motors and General Electric trading at around $35 per share. At those prices, you won't be buying many shares of each company before your investment budget is maxed out. Although mutual funds are not the favorite method of serious individual investors, they can be a good route to portfolio diversification if you don't have a lot of cash at your disposal.

Another approach to diversity is **asset allocation,** which spreads your risk even thinner by building a portfolio with fixed-income investments, such as bonds and cash, as well as equities such as stocks. Although returns are lower with this approach than if you invested solely in equities, it offers a lot more reassurance in unstable or over-leveraged markets. (See Chapter 10: Spotlight: The 2008 Collapse of the Financial Market and the Fate of the Big Banks.) Mutual fund managers are getting in on asset allocation by offering funds that allocate your investment money according to your goals and tolerance for risk. Look for descriptions like "life cycle fund," or "target date fund."

Long Term vs. Short Term Strategies

In more predictable periods in economic history, **buy and hold** was considered the sacred gospel of investing. This investment strategy instructs the investor to acquire stocks with the intent of owning them for a long time, typically at least 10 years, and ignoring movements up or down in the market. Although the initial selection of stocks is active, the approach becomes passive as soon as the buy is complete.

In contrast, **active trading** employs constant monitoring of the market in order to exploit short-term price changes by buying when the price is low and selling when it's high. The most active traders are the day traders, who revel in the speculative nature of their approach and thrive on the adrenaline and stress that goes with it.

Which one is better? As a retail investor, my default approach is buy and hold, but I incorporate some active trading methods as well, and I have developed my own style that suits me. I've read objective studies that have convinced me that longer time horizons produce the best gains, but there are some caveats to go with that. While today's stock market has produced record returns even after the financial crisis of 2008, I am skeptical of the idea that stock prices will continue to go up and up when they're already so high. I'm not alone in my skepticism – many financial experts have declared that 2008 killed buy and hold as a so-called safe strategy, after so many conservative investors lost money by holding on to stocks that never came back, even though the market as a whole did.

I'm no longer a strict buy and hold investor because the market today is far more diverse than it was 50 years ago, and some sectors perform differently from others during the same time frame. Also, there are more resources available to the retail investor nowadays than ever before. I've found it advantageous to use the internet to do my research, and to use online trading to manage my portfolio for the best gain based on current economic events. A pure buy and hold strategy seems more appropriate for the days of snail mail.

That said, I'm not the type of investor who loves the excitement of flipping stocks. It sounds glamorous to some, but it requires an obsessive dedication to the movements of the market, a brokerage account that charges an expensive monthly subscription fee instead of per transaction, and the ability and funds to track the stock exchanges in real time. It's a 24/7 job that requires a high degree of skill and experience – anything less can mean losing your shirt.

Fundamental Analysis vs. Technical Analysis

When picking stocks, investors tend to fall into two different camps: fundamental or technical.

Fundamental Analysis

This method consists of measuring the value of an investment by studying all of the factors that could affect it now or in the future. Fundamental analysis is the most mainstream method. As the name implies, this method studies the "fundamentals" of a security, be it a company or a mutual fund or a bond. The investor looks at the various metrics that indicate the health of the company before purchasing its stock.

Fundamental analysts study metrics like income, expenses, profit-and-loss, assets and liabilities, and anything related to the management and overall financial health of the investment. They also study larger financial conditions such as the state of the national and international economy, and conditions within the particular industry where the investment operates.

The company's price-to-earnings ratio is an important measurement. Some investors also analyze price-to-gross-sales ratio, while others include debt-to-equity ratios in their analysis. All of these metrics are basically ways to compare the performance of one company with other, similar companies. This method is generally more favored by long-term investors.

Technical Analysis

This method uses statistics and modeling to track patterns and trends from the past that might predict what an investment will do in the future. Those who prefer this approach tend to be shorter-term investors, or at least more active ones.

With this method, the fundamentals are irrelevant. Instead of calculating and comparing business metrics, technical analysis relies on the study of the statistics generated by the market itself. These metrics are usually expressed in graphic format, such as a stock chart. Analyzing the shape of the plot on the graph allows the technical analyst to predict future performance based on past performance numbers.

The technical analyst seldom relies on only one metric. Instead, a wide array of graphics is used to predict a company's performance. For example, one common method to assess growth is to pair the number of shares traded, called "volume," with share price.

Technical analysis is quite complex, and it's beyond the scope of this book to make you into an expert on it. If you'd like to learn more about it, I highly recommend *Traders World*, a quarterly publication that is respected by the experts in this method.

If you want to start an argument, walk into a roomful of traders and state a preference for either method – it doesn't matter which one! Both methods have their pros and cons. The strongest objection to fundamental analysis is the **efficient market hypothesis** (EMH) which claims that there are no truly undervalued stocks because the market efficiently causes share prices to reflect their true value at any given time. As a result, according to the EMH, analyzing the fundamentals is not going to bring you any returns higher than the current market rate. It sounds plausible, but Warren Buffet (see Chapter 6) would disagree, and he has about 55 billion reasons for his disagreement.

Technical analysts adopt a similar stance in arguing that their method is superior to fundamental analysis. They believe that the best indicator of a stock's potential is the price itself. For this reason, although there's no rule that says you can't use both methods, in practice investors seldom do.

Despite these objections, I use fundamental analysis on a regular basis because my approach is generally a longer-term one. For this reason, I recommend that you develop an understanding of it as you go about picking your stocks.

Fundamental Analysis: Evaluating a Company

The basic concept behind fundamental analysis is evaluating a company's stock price and deciding whether it represents the stock's true worth. That "true worth" figure is called "intrinsic value," which you determine by analyzing the fundamentals. The fundamentals can be anything that might indicate the economic strength or weakness of the company. If the stock is priced below its intrinsic value, it's a good investment. If it's priced higher, it probably isn't. Fundamental analysis assumes that over time, the market will come to reflect the stock's intrinsic value, although you might not know how long it will take the stock to reach that value.

The fundamentals are divided into two categories, "quantitative" and "qualitative." We'll look at each of them in depth for the rest of this chapter.

Quantitative fundamentals are factors that can be measured using numbers. The obvious source of quantitative data is the financial statements, so that's where we'll look first.

The Balance Sheet

This statement is a snapshot of a company's assets, liabilities and equity at a single point in time. The balance sheet formula is:

$$Assets = Liabilities + Shareholders'\ Equity$$

The balance sheet gets its name because the sections on either side of the = sign must match, or "balance." Assets are always listed in the first section and include any resource with value that the company owns – items like inventory, cash on hand, and real estate. The second section represents the money the company has borrowed to obtain those assets. One category is liabilities, which are debts that must be repaid. The second category is shareholders' equity, which is the money that investors have spent to buy a part of the company in the form of stock.

Most investors skip over the balance sheet and go directly to earnings, but you can learn a lot by looking at it. I look for companies with more assets than liabilities, and I'm especially interested in how much debt a company has. I also look at how the balance sheet changes from quarter to quarter and year to year. A sudden increase in debt can mean the company is investing in new products or programs that will bring in more revenue – or it can mean trouble. Either way, you will want to inquire further.

Another item I look for in the assets section is cash on hand. I like to see growth, and shrinking cash reserves are usually a red flag. I also take note if the company is sitting on a large pile of cash above and beyond a comfortable cushion for operations. Active companies invest their cash in pursuit of new opportunities. Another red flag is a large number of receivables, which are uncollected debts. Generally, a large number of payments uncollected after 90 days is the sign of a troubled industry.

The Income Statement

Income statements are compiled for a set period of time, such as a quarter or year, as opposed to the snapshot nature of the balance sheet. They examine three factors: revenue, expenses, and profit. The income statement formula is:

Profits = Revenue - Expenses

Revenue is money earned, usually through sales. Expenses are money spent, either to acquire inventory, or to run the company. Profit (or loss) is the difference between the two and is commonly expressed as "net profit," or the "bottom line" – that is, when all expenses of doing business have been subtracted from revenue.

71

When a company announces its quarterly profit or loss and its share price jumps up or down as a result, you're seeing the results of the numbers on the income statement.

The reason there's so much market focus on quarterly profit or loss is because the income statement is such an important metric for a company's success. Sure, there are success stories out there of companies like FedEx that lost money for several years before becoming wildly profitable, and I can think of a certain online retailer whose shareholders seem to have almost unlimited patience with meager or nonexistent profits. But it's a fact that a company that loses large amounts of money year after probably isn't going to be in business much longer, and therefore you don't want to buy its stock. One thing I look at especially closely on the income statement is the profit margin – the higher the difference between revenues and expenses, the better. Companies with razor-thin margins have to sell in much higher volumes to make money, which leaves them vulnerable to a rough patch in their industry.

One of the more interesting things about the market (or the strangest, some would say) is that even if a company makes a quarterly profit, its share price can fall if that profit was below expectations. An unexplained dip in a company's bottom line undermines investor confidence, so they take their investment dollars elsewhere. In the stock market, confidence isn't everything, but it's hard to do business without it.

The Statement of Cash Flows

This income statement examines the money flowing into and out of a company over a period of time. Cash flow is different from profit in that it includes borrowed funds as well as the company's own funds. Cash flow is the life blood of a company. A company can be profitable on paper according to the income statement, but without money to pay for its day to day expenses, its operations will immediately cease. The income statement is where all the flashy big numbers show up, but the cash flow statement is the bedrock. Take a close look at the free cash flow numbers. A healthy company has cash on hand to invest and to reward those who invest in it.

The cash flow statement is divided into three sections: cash flows from operations, financing and investing.

- **Operating Activities:** This section reflects how much cash is generated from sales after subtracting the cash needed to make those sales. I look critically at striking differences between the earnings on the income statement and cash flow from operations. If net income is high but cash flow is low, then the company may be recording its income or expenses in a way that doesn't reflect its true cash situation.

- **Investing Activities:** Any capital expenditures go here, such as money spent on new equipment, mergers and acquisitions, and investments. Look for capital re-investment as a sign of a healthy company that is actively pursuing opportunities for future growth.

- **Financing Activities:** This is the category for money raised from outside sources and can include loans the company obtains, and of course the sale of stock. This figure would go down if the company pays dividends, repurchases stock, or pays off a loan – all signs of a healthy operation.

Where to Find the Income Statements

Now that you've familiarized yourself with the financial statements, your next step is to go look them up. For stocks traded on any of the US exchanges, the Securities And Exchange Commission (SEC) maintains a database of each company's financial documents on its **Edgar** website.
http://www.sec.gov/edgar.shtml

Quarterly and annual filings are required of all companies that issue stock in the US. The annual filing is called the 10-K, and the quarterly filings are called the 10-Q. These documents are required because regulators believe that it's in everyone's best interest to keep a company's financial profile transparent so investors know what they're getting into if they buy shares of its stock. If a company prefers not to publicly disclose its financial dealings, it always has the option of foregoing public trading and instead relying on private investment funds.

- **The 10-K:** This is the annual statement that gets filed at the end of each fiscal year for the company. In addition to the three financial statements that I explain above, you can find a wealth of information about the company's operations. This can include historical financial data, biographical profiles of management, and long-term planning. Note that the 10-K is not quite the same as a company's annual report, although both contain the same financial information. Generally, the annual report is the 10-K published in glossy packaging and mailed to major investors as a promotional tool.

- **The 10-Q**: This is the smaller report that gets filed at the end of each of the first three fiscal quarters of the fiscal year. (The 10-K serves as the fourth quarterly report, as well as the annual report.) Note that unlike the 10-K, 10-Qs have no auditing requirement.

There are other sections of the 10-K and 10-Qs that you can use to evaluate the fundamentals of a company. The preamble to the financial statements is the **management discussion and analysis** (MD&A). There are no strict requirements for what goes into this section, so instead of looking at what it says, I tend to look at what it doesn't say. If I know about a downturn in the industry, or a challenge that the company faced in the past year, I prefer to see the company being candid about it. Obfuscation of the facts, or outright ignoring them, tells me that there's more going on behind the scenes than meets the eye. Similarly, I always check the 10-K to make sure it's been approved by an independent auditor.

Item 6. Selected Financial Data

SELECTED CONSOLIDATED FINANCIAL AND OPERATING DATA

The information set forth below should be read in conjunction with "Management's Discussion and Analysis of Financial Condition and Results of Operations" and our consolidated financial statements and the notes thereto.

	Fiscal Year Ended				
(dollars in millions except per share data)	Jan. 29, 2011	Jan. 30, 2010	Jan. 31, 2009	Feb. 2, 2008	Feb. 3, 2007(1)
Statement of Operations Data					
Sales(2)	$ 2,252.8	$ 2,679.9	$ 3,133.6	$ 3,439.9	$ 3,443.7
Operating loss(2)	$ (296.4)	$ (99.0)	$ (158.8)	$ (16.7)	$ (4.0)
Loss from continuing operations(2)	$ (300.3)	$ (112.5)	$ (192.1)	$ (31.2)	$ (28.1)
Income (loss) from operations of discontinued operations, net	$ (2.2)	$ 2.3	$ 5.7	$ 2.6	$ (123.2)
Gain (loss) from disposal of discontinued operations, net	$ 3.5	$ 0.8	$ (0.3)	$ (128.8)	$ —
Income (loss) from discontinued operations	1.3	3.1	5.4	(126.2)	(123.2)
Net loss	$ (299.0)	$ (109.4)	$ (186.7)	$ (157.4)	$ (151.3)
Per Share Data					
Diluted (basic) loss from continuing operations per common share(2)	$ (4.39)	$ (1.87)	$ (3.19)	$ (0.53)	$ (0.45)
Diluted (basic) gain (loss) from discontinued operations per common share	$ 0.02	$ 0.05	$ 0.09	$ (2.15)	$ (1.99)
Diluted (basic) net loss per common share	$ (4.37)	$ (1.82)	$ (3.10)	$ (2.68)	$ (2.44)
Cash dividends declared per common share	$ —	$ —	$ —	$ 0.44	$ 0.41
Balance Sheet Data					
Working capital — continuing operations(2)	$ (117.7)	$ 34.0	$ 48.7	$ (33.7)	$ 194.8
Working capital	$ (117.7)	$ 60.6	$ 77.5	$ 38.2	$ 127.7
Total assets — continuing operations(2)	$ 964.7	$ 1,347.9	$ 1,544.7	$ 2,064.6	$ 2,159.1
Total assets	$ 964.7	$ 1,425.2	$ 1,609.0	$ 2,302.7	$ 2,613.4
Short-term borrowings — continuing operations(2)	$ 215.3	$ 274.0	$ 329.0	$ 547.3	$ 347.0
Short-term borrowings	$ 215.3	$ 274.0	$ 329.0	$ 548.4	$ 542.0
Long-term debt, including current portion — continuing operations(2)	$ —	$ 4.8	$ 5.0	$ 5.2	$ 5.4
Long-term debt, including current portion	$ —	$ 4.8	$ 5.2	$ 5.6	$ 5.4
Long-term capital lease obligations, including current portion — continuing operations(2)	$ 2.6	$ 3.2	$ 2.0	$ —	$ 0.1
Long-term capital lease obligations, including current portion	$ 2.6	$ 3.2	$ 2.0	$ —	$ 0.4
Stockholders' equity (deficit)	$ (153.7)	$ 158.3	$ 263.1	$ 479.1	$ 644.0

(1) Our 2006 fiscal year consisted of 53 weeks.

(2) Excludes the results of discontinued operations (Borders Ireland Limited, Books etc., U.K. Superstores, Australia, New Zealand, Singapore and Paperchase).

23

Selected financial data from the 2011 10-K filing for the now-defunct Borders Group.

The **notes to the financial statements** contain the accounting methods, and the disclosure. For the accounting method, if it changes from year to year, I take a closer look to see why it might have changed to make sure it's not hiding something. The disclosures can be particularly helpful, if you're patient about reading the fine print. In contrast to the "at-a-glance" compilation of financial data in the statements, the notes can tell you a lot about the how and why behind the statements.

Next let's look at the **qualitative fundamentals**, which are the intangibles that can't be measured in numbers. Think of the word "quality," or the lack thereof. Is the product good? Is the board of directors qualified? Is the brand a household word? Although there's no SEC disclosure requirement for these things, and you can't represent them on a balance sheet, they make a tremendous difference in the success or failure of a company.

Qualitative fundamentals fall into two categories: those within the company, and those in the business environment where the company operates. Let's look at internal factors first.

A company's business model is a good place to begin. How does a company actually make its money? What does it sell? The introduction to its 10-K filing should tell you, or a visit to its corporate website. Some companies have very simple business models, like PepsiCo, which sells food products to consumers, restaurants, and institutions. Other times the business model is not so clear cut. For example, for many years the Big Three automakers considered a new vehicle sold when it was transferred to a dealership – not when a consumer actually bought and paid for it. This business model was an effective way of sweeping the increasing problem of inventory backlog under the rug – until there was no more room to sweep. (See Chapter 3, Spotlight: General Motors: Then and Now.)

Another part of your qualitative due diligence is making sure the company practices good corporate governance. The policies are found in the company's charter and bylaws and are designed to make sure that the company has the proper oversight so that it maintains high ethical standards and complies with all government regulations. These policies and regulations are designed to protect investors and shareholders from malfeasance by directors and officers. Look for a reasonable degree of transparency in the company's dealings with shareholders and other investors. Although your share may be small, you're considering whether to become part owner of this company by buying its stock, so how it treats its investors is important.

Another qualitative fundamental is the management team. It's no secret that management can make or break a company, but to really learn about the quality of management, you either have to work there or be a multimillion dollar investor who can get the attention of the higher-ups. Fortunately, there are a couple of other ways. Publicly traded companies host quarterly conference calls with the CEO that you can listen in on or read the transcript on sites like Morningstar http://www.morningstar.com Although you won't be able to take part in the Q&A, you can listen carefully to the conversation and read between the lines. As always, look for signs of obfuscation and deflection.

I also look for stock ownership on the part of the management team, which is a sign that they believe in their company enough to risk investing in it themselves. Finally, if a manager has worked for other companies, put some effort into tracking down his performance there. If he left under a cloud or was fired, and you believe that treatment was appropriate, then there's no reason to believe things will be any different in his new position.

You can also look at competitive advantage as a qualitative fundamental. Any successful company is going to have competition trying to grab its market share and take away some of its profit. A company that is dominant in its industry and is doing the right things to stay that way is going to be a better investment than an underdog, unless that underdog is taking aggressive steps to climb to the top.

Let's move on to qualitative factors outside of the company, in the business environment where it operates – the industry itself.

A company's customer base is an indicator of its strength in the marketplace. We've seen major manufacturers in the aerospace industry disappear overnight when government contracts dried up. It's better to invest in companies with a diverse customer base. You could argue that a company that sells to a large number of smaller customers is in better financial health than one that sells to a small number of large customers, but that's often the reality of consumer sales versus business-to-business sales. Nonetheless, the SEC requires that companies that rely on a single large customer for their revenue must disclose this fact in their 10-K filing.

What is the company's market share? This is related to competitive advantage above, but it also tells you something about the market itself. Is it up for grabs, with many companies competing for small slices of the pie, or does one player dominate above the rest? For example, in many US communities, four or five big-box retail locations are competing for a limited number of customers. The available market share isn't big enough to support that many competing stores, so it's inevitable that sooner or later, after operating at a loss for as long as they can, some of them are going to close. Apparently, the incredibly thin margins for consumer electronics aren't sufficient to scare away the competition.

Is the company positioned in a growth industry? Will there be more and more customers all the time, or fewer and fewer? Remember netbooks, and how they initially displaced laptop computers, but were then displaced themselves by tablets like the iPad? The tablet industry is clearly a growth industry, with more and more users buying hardware every year, but it took the right product to bring those users on board and make them customers. The netbook, an inferior product, didn't do the job.

Is the industry heavily regulated? For example, pharmaceuticals are definitely a growth industry, but the products are staggeringly expensive to research and develop, with costs in the hundreds of millions, and at least that amount once again to get the approval of the US Food and Drug Administration (FDA). The US pharmaceutical industry has developed many wildly successful drug products, but it has also lost billions on duds that didn't get approval or had to be withdrawn from the market.

In conclusion, with the right combination of quantitative and qualitative factors, fundamental analysis can give you an accurate picture of a company's overall health.

Chapter 6
Building Your Portfolio: How the Experts Do It

Although I don't rely on investment gurus to feed me the ticker symbols of the stocks I should buy, I do believe in learning the techniques of successful investors. I pay attention to investors who have maintained their success despite the high burnout rate in the world of professional investing, and the volatility of the market in 2008-2009 in which many investors lost millions of dollars. Sometimes it's talent; sometimes it's technique, and sometimes it's luck. Usually it's a combination of all three, but there's one thing that remains constant, and that's hard work and commitment. I'm happy to benefit from the learning experiences of the three investors profiled below.

Value Investing: Warren Buffett

Value investing is a strategy for choosing stocks that's closely tied to fundamental analysis. Value investors are the bargain hunters of the market, looking for stocks they believe are selling for less than their true worth and buying them hoping to make money when their value rises to reflect the company's true value (known as "intrinsic value" in fundamental analysis – see Chapter 5).

Warren Buffett made value investing a household word. With a 2013 net worth of over $55 billion, Buffett, who hails from

Nebraska, is known as the "Oracle of Omaha" for a good reason.

Buffett's approach to stock ownership is unconventional in that he looks beyond the stock market when evaluating the worth of a company. He believes in thinking of yourself as a partial owner of the business you invest in – because you are. This goes against the conventional wisdom that investors should maintain a distance from their portfolios to keep from becoming overly attached to any one stock. Buffett certainly doesn't advocate making investments on an emotional basis; in fact he actively discourages it. What he does recommend is developing a deep understanding of the companies and sectors that you invest in, just as if you were a business owner in that sector. For example, he avoids investing in tech stocks – not because he thinks tech is a bad investment, but because the in-depth knowledge he requires to invest in any given sector is limited by his available time.

It should already be obvious that Buffett's approach is a long-term, buy and hold strategy, but it goes far beyond share price or supply and demand. Buffett looks for companies with a solid business model that will make money and generate earnings for years to come. His philosophy reflects that of his mentor, Benjamin Graham, who famously said, "In the short run, the market is a voting machine but in the long run it is a weighing machine." Graham's meaning is that stocks reflect popularity in the short term and value in the long term. Buffett follows that advice by not allowing himself to get swept up in the ups and downs of the market, instead looking for great companies to invest in and believing that their share price will sort itself out over time.

Buffett employs fundamental analysis at an expert level that few can match. I can't hope to duplicate his entire formula in this book (even if there were space, Buffett has never shared that formula in its entirety), but I can list some of the main things he looks for.

- **Consistent performance over time:** Buffett analyzes shareholder return on equity (ROE) over a period of five to 10 years and compares it with other companies in that sector to gauge its performance. The formula is:

$$ROE = Net\ Income\ /\ Shareholder's\ Equity$$

- Buffett also looks at the length of time a company has been public and passes on those that had their IPO less than 10 years ago. He looks for long-term stable businesses whose share price he believes is below its true value. His genius lies in recognizing companies with good historical performance that will continue that performance – as opposed to those on a downward trend.

- **Avoidance of excessive debt:** Buffett's next metric is his preference for companies that rely on shareholder equity over debt for financing their growth. The formula is:

$$Debt/equity\ ratio = Total\ Liabilities\ /\ Shareholders'\ Equity$$

- A high ratio number indicates a higher reliance on debt, which generates interest expenses and relies on factors in the economy that are beyond the company's (and the investor's) control, such as interest rates.

- **High profit margins:** Buffett looks back at least five years for profit margins that are not only high, but constantly increasing. He considers this a sign of strong management. The formula is:

$$Profit\ margin = net\ income\ /\ net\ sales$$

- The higher the margin, the fewer expenses the company has as a cost of doing business.

- **Economic "moat":** In medieval times, the moat was a ring of water that protected the castle from invaders. Similarly, Buffett looks for companies with characteristics that set it apart from the competition, something other companies can't touch. For example, he subjects companies that rely on commodities to extra scrutiny, because commodities are by nature easy to replicate. A company with a competitive advantage not available to other companies will be able to do a better job of protecting its market share.

- **Stock selling at a 25% discount from the company's intrinsic value:** This is where the "value" part of value investing comes into play. The investor's job is to determine the intrinsic value of a company and then buy 25% lower. Buffett uses his own fundamental analysis formula consisting of qualitative and quantitative factors (see Chapter 5) and then compares it to the company's market cap. If his intrinsic value measurement comes in 25% higher than its market cap, he considers it a value investment. This is the most difficult part of the process.

In terms of an overall investment strategy, Buffett cautions against over-diversification. He feels that if an investor needs to hedge against losses by not committing to any one company, then he or she needs to do more homework and find a few companies that deserve a high level of commitment. Not surprisingly, he has absolutely no interest in investing in mutual funds!

Once Buffett finds a company that he feels is worth his investment dollars, he hangs on to its stock, in contrast to most investors who see a high share price as an opportunity to sell and realize a gain. Instead, if the company performs according to his expectations, he acquires more shares in it, believing that success breeds success. Another advantage of this long-term buy and hold approach is that it avoids transaction fees and capital gains taxes, which can be considerable when you're investing in the seven figure range.

My favorite part of Buffett's investment strategy is his concept of limited choices. He says we investors should make our decisions as if we only had 20 choices to use up, instead of the entire market to choose from. It shows a lot of discipline when you can avoid chasing after average or slightly above average investments and only take the bait if the prospect is exceptional. It really is a lot like life, isn't it?

Bond Expert: Bill Gross

Sometimes you can learn more from your mistakes than from doing it right (although it's a lot more pleasant if they're other people's mistakes, not yours). With the Dow again hitting 14,000, and the Federal Reserve threatening to taper off its quantitative easing bond purchases, the debt market hasn't been getting a lot of love from investors lately. The one exception is Bill Gross, who manages nearly $2 trillion in assets through the Pacific Investment Management Company (PIMCO). His fund is one of the world's largest, and Gross himself is widely regarded as the foremost authority on bond investment.

Gross's experience in 2013 is a prime example of learning from your mistakes – in his case, a very expensive mistake. Gross had been adding US Treasury bonds to PIMCO's various mutual fund portfolios, signaling confidence in the bond market at a time when other investors were growing increasingly wary.

To understand Gross's choices, it's important to understand how bonds work. (See Chapter 1.) Investors tend to run to the bond market when stocks seem too risky to invest in. When investors park their funds in treasuries and other bonds, demand goes up, so bond prices go up. However, since demand is high, yields, which are the interest payout on your investment, go down, and you make less money.

The US Federal Reserve has been heavily involved in the bond market since the financial crisis of 2008 through a practice called quantitative easing (QE). This unconventional monetary policy consists of the Fed buying mortgage-backed securities and long-term Treasuries to stimulate the economy. The reasoning goes that if yields on Treasuries and other bonds are low, banks will use their cash to make new loans, injecting the economy with much-needed cash for growth. The problem is that the Fed has to walk the thin, fine line between inflation and extremely low interest rates. If interest rates are so low that there's no incentive for banks to lend money, then all the QE in the world isn't going to force them to. However, if interest rates are too high, inflation results from too much money entering the economy at once.

Until 2013, the Fed pursued an aggressive QE strategy, and even initiated a second round, dubbed "QE2," in 2010. Bonds responded by performing extraordinarily well. Then in 2013, Ben Bernanke, head of the Federal Reserve, had what the pundits dubbed a "taper tantrum," threatening to taper off quantitative easing that year. Instead of treating bonds as a long-term investment, investors feared an increased in prices paired with a reduction in yields and started frantically dumping their bonds.

Meanwhile, Bill Gross was buying long-term Treasuries for PIMCO. His prediction was that the US economy was too sluggish for Bernanke to undertake any serious tapering in QE bond purchases. He was correct, but he forgot that in the financial markets, perception is everything – at least in the short term. In June 2013, PIMCO's Total Return Fund nosedived by 4%, after increasing by an impressive 7% over the previous five years. Investors responded by pulling their assets out of the fund, giving PIMCO an unwelcome haircut.

This unexpected black eye prompted Gross to write a rather entertaining letter to PIMCO's investors that began with the never-before-told story of how he almost sunk a navy ship as a 23-year-old officer. He then went on to explain PIMCO's losses by saying, "The U.S. economy is not sinking, nor are the majority of global economies. Their markets just had too much risk. In effect, the ship was top heavy with too little ballast. Guess I should have known, huh?"

In effect, Gross was declaring that long-term Treasuries aren't the *Titanic,* and any appearance that they were would be short-lived. He echoed statements by Bernanke himself in predicting that inflation would need to rise above 2% and unemployment would have to dip below 6.5% before the Federal Reserve would start tapering down its QE bond purchases.

He was close. As of early 2014, inflation had edged slightly above 1.5%, and unemployment fell to 6.7%, signaling a possible end to the sluggishness that had plagued the economy since 2008. On December 18, 2013, Bernanke announced that the Fed's purchases of Treasuries would be reduced by 12%, from $45 billion to $40 billion, beginning in January 2014. He lobbed a parting shot at the bond market on January 29, 2014, by further reducing that figure to $35 billion. His successor, Janet Yellen, will control future the future tapering of QE – if it happens at all. The US economy is still too unstable to predict whether QE will continue.

Gross's experience in 2013 was a great example of how uncertainty in the market can hurt even the most highly regarded investor. Treasuries have long been considered one of the safest investments, but with the Fed using them as a tool to manage an unsteady economy, they have become subject to market forces beyond even the best manager's control. *Kiplinger* pretty much summed things up when they said, "Bill Gross may be the best bond fund manager on the planet—just not in 2013."

Distressed debt wizard Howard Marks (see below) also weighed in on bonds in his November 2013 Oaktree Memo, stating that while the rest of the US economy has managed to avoid a bubble like the one in 2008, "the exception is bonds in general, which the central banks are supporting at yields near all-time lows, meaning prices near all-time highs. But I don't find them scary (unless their duration is long), since – if the issuers prove to be money-good – they'll eventually pay off at par, erasing the interim mark-downs that will come when interest rates rise."

If you want to invest in Treasuries, Gross recommends watching the interplay of price and yield for the US 10-Year Treasury Note while keeping an eye on US economic indicators. As long as the economy remains stagnant, the Fed is unlikely to raise the prime interest rate on loans. After that, it's a matter of buying when the price is low while the yield is reasonable, and hanging in there until they mature.

My favorite way to invest in Treasuries is through an ETF, which mixes up various Treasuries of varying maturity periods. If you're willing to give him a second chance, Gross's own PIMCO has a diverse ETF with a mix of private, municipal, and Treasury bonds that fared better in 2013 than his Total Return Fund. Appropriately, it trades on the NASDAQ with the ticker symbol BOND.

Predicting Risk: Howard Marks

Howard Marks made his mark on the investment world by investing in distressed debt. He founded Oaktree Capital Management in 1995, and since then the company has outperformed the stock market, as well as most of its peers in the distressed debt sector, by averaging an annual return of 19% after fees. Oaktree raised over $10 billion during the financial crisis of 2008 to acquire distressed assets – and there were many to choose from. The result was successful enough that the company went public in 2012.

Marks is a prolific and thoughtful writer. His "Oaktree Memos" have achieved mythical status in the investment world due to their simplicity and the way Marks clearly conveys complex ideas in plain language. He's generous about sharing his wisdom with others, and all of the memos can be read free of charge on his website, http://www.oaktreecapital.com/memo.aspx

In November 2013, Marks's Oaktree Memo, "The Race Is On," offered an in-depth look at the degree of risk in the current investing environment, and whether the factors that led up to the financial crisis of 2008 were repeating themselves. http://www.oaktreecapital.com/MemoTree/The%20Race%20Is%2 0On_2013_11_26.pdf I have read this memo at least a dozen times since its release, and I'll read it a dozen times more. In mid-2007, Marks had predicted the causes (although not the severity, he admits) of the Great Recession with stunning accuracy in his memo, "The Race to the Bottom," and he sees many of the same behaviors rearing their ugly heads again as the stock market climbs and investors regain their confidence. He concludes that it's not time to bail out of the market – at least, not yet – but that wise investors will keep a close eye on the factors he lists in the memo and allocate their assets accordingly.

The structure of this memo is a side-by-side comparison of today's investing picture with that of 2007, both the similarities and differences. The primary similarity that Marks points out is investor tolerance for risk. He remarks that this tolerance began surprisingly quickly after the crisis of 2008 had passed (which he first pointed out in his memo of May 2010), and he lays the blame at the feet of the Federal Reserve for pursuing policies that depressed the return on safe investments. As you might guess, Marks is not a fan of quantitative easing; while he's not strictly anti-regulation, he thinks that QE is too novel and unpredictable to be a safe tool for managing market outcomes. (As I mention above, the 2013 performance of Bill Gross's PIMCO fund is a prime example of why Marks has a point.)

Marks is dismayed by the current emphasis on momentum investing over solid fundamentals, but he refuses to get emotional about it. He simply sees it as a metric of the risk level in the current environment. In his November 2013 memo he states, "When people start to posit that fundamentals don't matter and momentum will carry the day, it's an omen we must heed." He understands that the more risk investors are willing to take, the more pressure it places on the risk-averse investor to join the race because the only alternative is to be excluded from returns altogether. Meanwhile, as more and more investors move toward riskier investments, the entire financial market becomes more unsteady.

"I believe most strongly that the riskiest thing in the investment world is the belief that there's no risk," he continues. With surgical precision and detachment, he lists the 2013 factors that he believes are preventing another 2008, at least so far. He lists these factors in bullet point form, but the one thing they all have in common is uncertainty. He believes that nearly all investors are aware of the looming questions surrounding the financial market today, questions that are so numerous that they take two pages to cover in the memo. He then points out that they are nonetheless pursuing risky investments because the returns on safe investments are so poor that they have very little choice. Thus, the race to the bottom is on once again.

Marks stops short of saying it's time to sell – he simply recommends heightened caution. In the memo he paraphrases Warren Buffett's thoughts on the matter: "When others are acting imprudently, making the world a riskier place, our caution level should rise in response." As conditions in the market change, we can expect future memos from Oaktree to inform us of those changes – and I for one will be studying them in detail.

Chapter 7
Time to Invest

You've done a lot of learning in the first half of this book. Now it's time to put it to good use. In this chapter, you will learn how and where to buy stocks.

Trading Simulators on the Web

Trading simulator websites are an excellent way to get a feel for how the stock market works and how stock values can change. They allow you create your own investment account with the stock picks of your choice. Most of them are free to join. The simulator delivers a daily report for each stock and an aggregated report for your portfolio, so you can see how your simulated investment is doing.

These sites are loads of fun. It's all play money, so there's nothing to lose. Here are some sample sites.

- Wall Street Survivor: http://www.wallstreetsurvivor.com/

- How the Market Works:
  http://www.howthemarketworks.com/

- Investopedia Stock Simulator:
  http://simulator.investopedia.com/

- Young Money: http://finance.youngmoney.com/stock-market-game/

- Marketwatch:

http://www.marketwatch.com/game/?link=MW_Nav_GA

- National SMS: http://www.nationalsms.com/

You can also search popular application sites like iTunes and Amazon.com, using keywords like "stock market simulator," if you want to play on your handheld device.

Choosing a Broker

A broker is a licensed professional who agrees to keep your money in an account and invest it according to your wishes, for a fee. Until the Securities and Exchange Commission (SEC) deregulated brokers in 1975, all brokerages were full-service brokerages, and fees and commissions were uniform no matter which firm you went to. After deregulation, the discount brokerage firm was born, and the retail investor was the lucky beneficiary.

Full-Service Brokers

Full-service brokerage firms tout services that the discount brokers don't offer. The most common of these is extensive investment advice and financial forecasting using teams of analysts and economic experts. While the investor handling millions of dollars of other people's money probably wants to point to these experts when reporting to his clients, the retail investor should think carefully about whether they are worth the high price.

The other factor that marks a full-service broker is working on commission. There could be significant pressure in these firms to make as many trades as possible to keep commissions coming in.

Discount Brokers

Discount brokers manage your funds but don't provide advice. They work at a lower overhead than full-service brokers, so they charge far less. Not surprisingly, the number of discount brokers has grown exponentially, while the number of full-service brokers has shrunk. Many discount brokerage employees work on salary, so, while transactions still generate fees for the company, the additional incentive to maximize trades is missing.

Choosing a discount broker will depend on whether you want to do business with an office in your location, or conduct your trades online. Although their fees are generally reasonable, be sure to inquire closely about what exactly you'll be paying for, how much, and how often. For example, most brokerages offer their own proprietary mutual fund packages with a minimal brokerage fee. If you want to buy shares of a fund managed by another brokerage through your own broker, be sure to ask whether there's an additional fee to do this.

Discount brokers offer all of the investment securities and services discussed in this book, including:

- Stocks
- Mutual funds
- Money market funds
- Index funds
- Exchange traded funds (ETFs)
- Dividend stocks
- Dividend Reinvestment Plans
- Automatic deposits

Online Brokers

Internet trading offers even lower fees than discount brokers, which makes it attractive to many investors. I was initially attracted by the freedom of managing my own investments without having to go through a broker, and the low fees for trading.

Those low fees have a down side, though. They make it easy to get caught up in the wheeling and dealing aspect of the stock market and lose sight of investing for the long term. The ease of pushing a button and making a trade meant that I woke up one day and found I had spent more, not less money on fees than I spent with a discount broker. My monthly online brokerage statement was a wakeup call for me to reevaluate my trading habits and refocus on my commitment to stable, long-term investments.

Signing Up for a Discount Brokerage

So you're all done with play money and are ready for the real thing? As a beginning investor, you will probably start with a discount brokerage. Many of the big-name discount brokers offer both online and in-person trading options in an effort to retain as many customers as possible. Some of the large players in the discount brokerage field include:

- Fidelity

- WellsTrade

- Merrill Edge

- Scottrade

- Firstrade

- Schwab

- Etrade (the best known of the online discount brokerage houses)

Your initial question when shopping for a broker is whether the office you are dealing with is the actual broker, or a company selling services for a broker. Broker-resellers aren't automatically a bad idea, but with so many brokerages offering direct services, why take a chance?

There is a minimum deposit requirement for opening a brokerage account, usually between $500 and $1,000. This is still your money, just as it would be in a bank account.

You should also know the difference between a cash account and a margin account. A cash account is limited to your initial deposit plus any earnings from sales of stock or dividends, while a margin account allows you to borrow money from the brokerage to purchase stock. Margin accounts can be risky. If the share price falls drastically, you can get hit with a "margin call," where the brokerage dips into your account and sells your investments to cover the loan.

Understanding Transaction Costs

A key term or set of terms to understand before you call or click on your brokerage account is **bid-ask spread.** This affects the price at which you will be able to buy shares of a stock you want to add to your portfolio and therefore your portfolio's total return on your investment:

- **Bid:** The highest price that you, the buyer, are willing to pay for a share.

- **Ask:** The lowest price at which the seller is willing to sell you that share.

- **Bid-Ask Spread:** The difference between the bid and the ask. For instance, if your bid price is $101, and the ask price is $100, then the bid-ask spread is $1. The spread can vary, depending on how often a share is traded. Currency assets and large-company stocks change hands on a daily basis, so their spread is very low; while stocks with fewer shares or a lower trading volume may have a higher spread.

The recipient of the spread amount is the market maker, sometimes called a specialist, who pockets the difference between the bid and the ask as profit. The market maker plays a vital role in the marketplace by keeping stocks liquid at all times, ready to be bought and sold. Generally, the higher the demand for a stock, the lower the spread, since more market makers are needed to handle the demand, so competition increases among them.

Remember that the bid-ask spread is separate from your broker's commissions and fees, which are another cost. Added up together, they represent your total transaction costs for your stock purchase. You need to be aware of these costs and make sure they stay at a level you can accept, but they're a fact of life and a cost of doing business in the market. When you purchase a stock at the ask price, its value in your portfolio is actually the bid price, since the difference goes to the maker. Before you start wringing your hands in despair over losing money right away, remember that the spread is only a loss if you plan to turn around and sell your shares right away. Since the whole point of buying stock is to hold it long enough to make money through capital appreciation and/or dividends, you should be able to absorb your transaction costs as your portfolio increases in value.

Keeping Brokerage Fees Under Control

The usual sales pitch for a discount brokerage lists their lowest fee as a selling point. If this number is higher than $10, it probably isn't a discount broker, but keep in mind that it's only a fraction of the story. From there, prices go up, and the methodology for calculating them can become quite confusing. Some brokerages charge a monthly fee, while others charge a fee per transaction. If you're an active investor who makes frequent trades, look for monthly fees. Passive investors should opt for a fee per transaction agreement while looking closely for minimum monthly trade requirements.

In either case, you need to look at the fee agreements *very* carefully before you sign up and make sure your broker answers your questions. Any signs of evasion or hard-sell tactics are good reasons to take your business elsewhere.

Placing an Order

Ready to buy or sell? It's time to learn about the types of orders you, as an individual investor, can place with your broker. There a several different types of orders, but the ones I list below are among the most useful. Keep in mind that whether you are buying or selling a stock, both transactions are called orders in the lingo of the marketplace because you're giving your broker instructions.

- **Market Order:** This tells your broker to immediately buy or sell a stock at the best price currently available. Since you haven't placed a limit on the price or the time in which the order can be carried out, these orders are considered unrestricted. That means a lower-volume stock could have a much higher ask price than the current market price displayed on your stock chart, resulting in considerable sticker shock when you see the spread you just paid for. With higher-volume, in-demand stocks, a market order is safer and can result in some savings on broker commissions since there is little work involved.

- **Limit Order:** Here you tell your broker to stick to a certain price limit. If you set a limit of $20 per share, then your broker will only buy this stock for you if the ask price is $20 or less; and he will only sell it for you at a bid of $20 or more. You can further limit your broker's options by specifying a time limit. A day order will be canceled if your price limit isn't met on the same day. A good-till-canceled (GTC) order remains in effect until it is either filled, or you deliberately cancel it with your broker. And a fill-or-kill order must be fulfilled right away for the entire number of shares you ordered, or it gets canceled. Broker commissions on limit orders and other orders with time and price constraints tend to be higher than for market orders.

- **Stop Order:** Also known as a stop-loss order, this sets a predetermined entry point for a buy, or an exit point for a sale. If and when the stock reaches this point, your order converts to a market order. The intent of a stop order is to lock in your profit and protect yourself from loss, but it doesn't always work that way. Your entry or exit point is only a benchmark. For example, if the price dips lower than your exit point, the sale will still execute, at a lower price than you intended. One way to avoid this is to place a stop limit order instead, which allows you to cut off the sale if it exceeds the range you specify. Stop orders and stop limit orders can be placed as day orders, good-till-canceled, or fill-or-kill, just like a limit order.

- **Trailing Stop Order:** This allows you to track the direction of a stock's price automatically and sell if its price goes down by more than a certain percentage compared with the price you paid for it. By setting a good-till-canceled trailing stop at, for example, 10 percent of the purchase price, you can sit back and ignore minor, single-digit fluctuations in the marketplace and only sell the stock if it continues on a downward trend. I use trailing stops extensively as a way of protecting my investment dollars and getting rid of stocks that aren't performing as I expect. However, I keep an eye on items in my portfolio that are approaching my stop cutoff percentage. If it looks like the downward trend is only temporary, due to something transient like a temporary decline in the availability of a raw material, or a political situation that has been resolved, then I might set my stop percentage higher. And in the spirit of Warren Buffett's philosophy of value investing (see Chapter 7), I might even place an order for more shares of the same stock and take advantage of the low price!

Chapter 8
Introduction to Dividend Investing

Why You Should Learn About Dividends

I learned about dividend investing while I was still in a growth investing mindset, and I believe that most beginning investors are in the same position. So I'm going to start by explaining the differences between the two.

Growth Investing vs. Dividend Investing

Investing for growth means buying stocks in the hope that their share price will go up after you buy them. The old saying, "buy low and sell high," is an apt description. Investing for growth means you don't make any profit from your stocks until you actually sell them – and only if you can sell them at a higher price per share than you paid for them.

Dividend investing is sometimes called "investing for income" because dividend stocks pay you income on a regular basis (usually quarterly), regardless of their share price. Not all stocks pay out dividends, but at first glance, dividend stocks look just like any other stock. They're publicly traded on the major indexes, and you buy your shares through your brokerage account. Sometimes their price per share goes up, and sometimes it goes down. As a dividend investor, you will want to "buy low," just as a growth investor would, but once you own the stock, any growth in share price is added to the fact that it's likely to pay dividends for as long as you own the stock.

Dividend Investing vs. Buy and Hold

At first glance, dividend investing looks a bit like the conservative "buy and hold" strategy so beloved of financial gurus, but there are important differences. The growth investor buys and holds with the aim of selling his shares for more than he paid for them at some point in the future and profiting from that sale. That approach is based on the assumption that the stock market will always recover after a downturn, and that, over a period of many years, stock prices will always increase in value at a rate that outpaces inflation (see Chapter 5).

Historically this may be true, but the volatility of the stock market in the twenty-first century has made many people skeptical – myself included. Since the year 2000, there have been two major downturns in the market – one in 2002, and one in 2008. I guess it's not politically correct to call them "crashes," but trust me, watching helplessly as your portfolio loses one-third to one-half of its value feels a lot like being in an automobile accident in slow motion.

It's true that both times the market recovered and went on reach historic highs. But the bear markets of the twenty-first century left a bad taste in many investors' mouths. We no longer take it as an article of faith that the market will always recover after a downturn, and we are approaching growth investing with a newfound caution.

I invest heavily in dividend stocks for four reasons:

1. When stock prices are high, dividends add to my income
2. When stock prices are low, dividends help me maintain my income
3. Whether stock prices are high or low, dividends help me

101

lower my risk

4. In 2012, the tax rate on dividends was 0% in my tax bracket, with a 15% maximum. As of early 2014, the maximum tax rate on dividends has gone up to 20%, but their tax rate in my income bracket (below $400,000 per year) continues to be 0%. These figures will hold until US tax policy is renegotiated by Congress.

Two Ways That Dividends Can Work for You

Suppose you had invested $10,000 in dividend stocks on the Dow Jones index at the beginning of 2000. Even with two major downturns in the market over the next 10 years, your dividends at the end of 2010 would probably surprise you.

- **Cash payments:** even if you simply took your dividends as cash deposits and spent them to support your lifestyle, from the moment you purchased the stock, the regular income would start to add up over time.

- **Reinvestment:** if you had used your dividends to purchase more shares of the same stocks, then those additional shares would also pay out dividends. Over a period of ten years, your income would compound to many times the original value of the cash dividends.

I hope you're starting to see why I'm such a cheerleader for dividends.

What Is a Dividend?

When a company makes a net profit after expenses at the end of a set period (such as a quarter), it can choose what to do with that money. A company with a policy of paying dividends will distribute some or all of its net profit to its shareholders, usually as a cash payment (although in some instances, dividends are paid out as stock shares instead).

All companies that pay dividends have two things in common:

- **Publicly traded:** Dividends are calculated according to a company's "shares outstanding" (the total number of shares currently owned by shareholders), so it needs to have publicly issued its stock.

- **Declaration of dividends:** the board of directors must make an official declaration that it will pay dividends for the upcoming period.

What about companies that *don't* pay dividends? Typically, they will hang on to any profits they make and reinvest them in the company to fuel rapid growth. That's why fast-growing market sectors, such as technology and alternative energy firms, seldom pay dividends. In contrast, older, more established companies that have already gone through their intensive growth phases are more likely to pay dividends.

How Are Dividends Calculated?

Dividends are calculated separately for common stock and preferred stock. Since this is book is for beginners, who are unlikely to obtain preferred stock, I will focus only on common stock dividends.

Here are the steps in the process for determining the payout per share for a dividend stock:

- **Payout ratio:** The board of directors examines the company's financial data and makes a decision on how much of its net profit to retain for operational costs and future investment vs. how much to pay out as dividends. The ratio of these two figures is called the "payout ratio."

- **Calculation:** The payout ratio is applied to the company's net profit to determine the total pot of money available to be paid out as dividends. This total is divided by the company's number of shares outstanding to arrive at the dividend per share (DPS). The formula for calculating the DPS is:

    total dividend payout divided by total shares outstanding.

- **Declaration:** The board of directors officially "declares" the DPS in an official resolution.

In addition there is some investor terminology that you should be familiar with if you're going to invest in dividend stocks:

- **Earnings per share (EPS):** This metric doesn't really tell you much by itself, but it's necessary for figuring out the P/E ratio. The formula for calculating a company's EPS is: *net profit* divided by *total shares outstanding*. For example, a company with earnings of $2.19 million and 292,000 outstanding shares would have an EPS of $7.50. EPS can be expressed in its basic form, or in its diluted form, which subtracts various stock options that might turn into common stock.

- **Price to earnings ratio (P/E ratio):** This metric measures the value of a stock by comparing how much it costs with how much it earns. Most stock charts display this figure prominently. The formula for calculating the P/E ratio is: *price per share* divided by *earnings per share in the past year*. For example, if the company above with an EPS of $7.50 is selling for $69 per share, its P/E ratio would be 9.2 (69 / 7.5 = 9.2).

- **Dividend yield (yield):** This measures the ratio of a stock's price per share to its dividend per share. It is always expressed as a percentage. The formula for calculating yield is: *dividend per share* divided by *share price*.

How Are Dividends Paid Out?

Dividends are almost always paid out on a quarterly basis, so to make things simple, I will operate under that assumption throughout this book.

The formula for calculating dividend payout is: *dividend per share* multiplied by *number of shares you own*. If you own 500 shares of a stock with a DPS of .05375 cents, then your dividend for that quarter is $26.88.

There are some dates in the life cycle of a quarterly dividend that you should know.

- **Date of declaration:** This is the date that the board of directors issues its resolution declaring a dividend.

- **Ex-dividend date:** three days before the date of record is the cutoff date for you to call your broker to purchase the stock so you can receive the dividend.

- **Record date:** three days after the ex-dividend date, your broker must finalize your stock purchase so you appear on the company's record books and can receive the dividend.

- **Distribution date:** The date the dividend is actually paid out.

Next we'll talk about how to find dividend stocks.

How to Find Dividend Stocks

There's no single comprehensive list of stocks that pay dividends, so finding them takes a bit of detective work. I find this both challenging and rewarding. I get a bit of a thrill each time I dig up a great buy on a dividend stock that the financial wizards have missed.

Check the Indexes

Let's start with the obvious places to look, and that's the indexes. An index is a survey of the stock market compiled by an index company. Indexes consist of a limited number of stocks that the index company believes represents the performance of the entire market. Most of the major indexes also compile several sub-indexes, which are based on particular sectors of the market, such as utilities, or biotechnology. Other sub-indexes track companies that pay dividends.

Major indexes in the US include:

- Dow Jones Industrial Average (DJIA)

- Standard & Poor's 500 (S&P500)
- NASDAQ: Although the NASDAQ is best known as a stock exchange, it also maintains several indexes.

Out of these three, the DJIA and the S&P500 are the ones you want to focus on. The NASDAQ indexes are heavily weighted toward emerging technologies, where companies prefer to retain their profits and invest them in future growth. Older, more established companies are more likely to pay dividends.

The DJIA and the S&P500 completed a formal merger in 2012 to become the S&P Dow Jones Indices. Both indexes are loaded with older companies, many of which pay dividends. In fact, the S&P500 actually publishes a list of "Dividend Aristocrats," consisting of companies it tracks that have increased their dividends every year for the past 25 years. The Aristocrats list is a great place to start shopping for dividend stocks. You can find it on the web at http://us.spindices.com/indices/strategy/sp-500-dividend-aristocrats

As you become more advanced in your dividend investing, you might want to look at the Value Line Dividend Select index at http://www.valueline.com/, which compiles dividend stocks from over 1,600 companies. The service has a two-week free trial.

Read the Publications

Most of the major financial publications are now web-based, so you don't have to buy print copies or dig them up in libraries. Although most of them keep their really good financial data behind a paywall, you can get a head start on digging up dividend stocks by going to the free part of their websites and searching for information on dividend stocks. Here is a partial list to get you going:

- Wall Street Journal
- Financial Times
- Forbes
- Investor's Business Daily

- Barron's

Check Online Stock Quotes

The major online stock ticker websites include search features to screen for stocks that pay dividends. Here are some of the best known:

- Yahoo! Finance: find your way to the Stock Screener page and set up a custom screen for dividend stocks. You can also subscribe to their "Dogs of the Dow" preset stock screener newsletter. The "Dogs" is a list of the top ten DJIA stocks with the highest dividend yield.

- Google Finance: this search engine's stock screener will let you set a minimum and maximum percentage range for dividend yield.

- AOL Daily Finance: also has a stock screener tool.

- Morningstar: although best known for analyzing mutual funds and ETFs, this site also has financial data on thousands of stocks, including some that pay dividends.

Note also that all of these sites allow you to type in a company's stock ticker symbol (usually expressed as 3 to 5 capital letters) and pull up a chart with lots of useful data for evaluating its financial health and future.

Get the Official Scoop

All publicly traded companies must file quarterly data with the Securities and Exchange Commission (SEC). These documents are extremely detailed and are available for free at www.sec.gov

Ask an Expert

If you already have a fiduciary relationship with a broker, then get his or her input. You should still do your own due diligence and research your broker's advice, but an investment specialist can help you narrow down your list of possible picks.

I like to keep track of potential picks in a spreadsheet so I can sort them out later. I keep it simple on my first pass and limit my record keeping to ticker symbol, dividend yield, and P/E ratio. It's easy to pull the ticker symbol off my list and use it to get more detailed information after I've narrowed down my prospects.

Risk Assessment and Management | Managed Funds | Dividend Reinvestment Plans | Real Estate Investment Trusts

Risk Assessment and Management

Growth investment is based on the assumption that the overall trend of the market is always upward, despite temporary downturns. Recently, more and more investors have started to question that assumption. In early 2013, the DJIA broke the 14,000 mark, yet investors remained remarkably cool about further involvement in the market. After two vicious bear markets within six years of each other, we've become quite risk-averse.

Among dividend investors there's a counterpart to the assumption of perpetual growth, and that's the assumption that companies that paid dividends in the past will always continue to do so in the future. And that brings us to a question.

Do Companies Ever Stop Paying Dividends?

Sure they do. The financial crisis of 2008 turned a lot of things upside down. If you had stock in General Motors when it declared bankruptcy, you not only didn't get a dividend, but the stock itself became worthless virtually overnight. This is shocking considering that GM was once the largest publicly traded company in the *world*. Other companies also took a beating in 2008, and when the dust had cleared, several companies that had spent years on the S&P500's Aristocrats list were no longer paying dividends, while others had greatly reduced their payout.

That said, companies don't like to reduce their dividend amount. It's an issue of perception – the market will interpret it as a sign of weakness, just as if its quarterly profits had fallen short of expectations, and investors will invest their funds elsewhere.

The rationale for dividends explains why they tend to be more stable than growth stocks. Companies that offer dividends are usually older companies that have completed their growth cycles, so they can no longer lure investors with tantalizing possibilities of astronomical growth in share price. Paying dividends is a way for these companies to ensure they have sufficient capitalization from investors, who see these stocks as a steady source of income that's less risky than growth stocks.

Some of the market sectors that tend to pay dividends include:

- **Utilities:** companies that sell power and fuel directly to the public

- **Energy:** producers of oil and gas

- **Telecoms:** both wired and wireless

- **Consumer products:** food, beverages, and household products

- **Pharmaceuticals**

SPOTLIGHT: HOW TO GET THE BEST RETURN FROM THE DOGS OF THE DOW

Sometimes investment strategies that go by catchy-sounding names turn out to be so much hot air. Not so with the Dogs of the Dow (http://dogsofthedow.com/), the classic investment strategy that has withstood the test of time since its creator, Michael B. O'Higgins, unveiled it in 1991.

The "Dogs" strategy is simple but effective. Each year you evaluate the 30 stocks in the Dow Jones Industrial Average index and buy the top 10, the ones with the highest dividend yields. In practice, this usually amounts to yields of 3% or better.

Investing in the Dogs will of course give you higher dividends, but there's more to it than that. The principle behind this strategy is to use a company's dividend yield to gauge the likelihood of its share price increasing. The rationale is that companies that pay dividends do not like to change their dividend per share much even if their stock price takes a nosedive. Remember that dividend yield is the ratio of a stock's price per share to its dividend per share. Therefore, a company with a high yield – that is, a high dividend but a low stock price – is probably at a low point in its share price cycle and is likely to see an increase in the upcoming year. When the strategy works, the investor gets a two-fer: already-high dividends plus appreciating share price.

Averaged out over time, the Dogs of the Dow have performed well – sometimes amazingly well. O'Higgins' research data shows the Dogs matching or outperforming the market consistently since 1920. That doesn't mean the strategy was a winner every year, but analyzed in 20-year chunks, or even 10-year and 5-year chunks, its performance has been good. Sometimes all 10 of the Dogs performed well; while in other years, two or three of them provided dazzling returns and made up for the others that behaved like...well, like dogs.

The worst years for the Dogs of the Dow are boom years and bust years. During the dot-com boom of the late 1990s, capital gains for tech stocks were so high that they eclipsed the more stable blue-chip stocks that paid out dividends. I held on to my dividend stocks during those years because I knew the party couldn't last, but I also invested in companies with growth trends in their share prices that I believed would still be around in the next century. Similarly, the financial crisis of 2008 knocked the bottom out of so many companies that their dividend yield was no longer a meaningful way to gauge which of them would recover.

I'm also a big fan of the Small Dogs of the Dow, which are the five Dogs with the lowest share price. The fact that the Small Dogs perform a good 2% better than the regular Dogs, and the Dow itself, tells me that there's something to O'Higgins's strategy.

One thing to be aware of if you're investing for growth is that some of the Dogs get on the list due to a high dividend price, rather than their share price growth potential. In order for the strategy to work, the stock has to move *off* the Dogs list at some point as its price goes up and its dividend-to-price ratio goes down. The reality is, many stocks on the list have been there for one or even two years, suggesting that their prices are remaining stagnant.

Nonetheless, investing in the Dogs of the Dow is an attractive way to choose which blue-chip stocks to put into your portfolio. You need some blue chips anyway, so why not take advantage of a strategy that's proven itself over time and enjoy the double benefit of high dividends and the possibility of capital appreciation in the near future?

Chapter 9
Advanced Dividend Investing

Evaluating Risk

After spending a miserable year glued to my computer screen gathering data in an attempt to become an active trader, I've come to appreciate buy and hold as an investment strategy. Nonetheless, you need to do your homework on a company before making a buy, so I'm going to lay out the process I use to conduct some basic due diligence before I buy a dividend stock.

On my first pass, I set my online stock screener tool to filter for companies with a dividend yield of greater than 3%. I enter the ticker symbol, yield percentage, and P/E ratio for each stock into my spreadsheet and sort for the best combination of yield and P/E ratio.

From the companies that score high in both categories, I pick the top ten and dig a little bit deeper in my research. Things I look for include:

- Has the company paid out a steady or increasing dividend every year for at least the past 10 years?

- Did the company actually make a profit each year it paid dividends? I don't want to invest in a company that's planning on liquidating.

- Is there any emerging technology that would make the

company obsolete? I try to avoid companies with complicated business models that I don't understand well enough to predict their future.

- Is the company's dividend yield *too* high? If the yield is high because the share price is low, then I want to know why their stock is so cheap. It might be a great deal, but it might also have lost value for a good reason.

Beyond this basic screening process, research on a company can be as in-depth as you like, depending on your tolerance for risk and the amount of money you're going to invest. As you build skill and confidence, I encourage you to construct your own research strategy that you enjoy using, one that works for your needs.

Dividends and Share Price

If a company passes inspection from an income investing perspective, I then look at it from a growth perspective. In the current bull market, it's pretty hard to find a good value investment – that is, a company with a low share price that pays a healthy dividend. And it's becoming harder all the time as risk-averse investors are flocking to dividend investing in an attempt to find a shred of stability in the market. No matter how tempting a high dividend yield might be, I avoid paying too much for an overpriced stock that's unlikely to go up and more than likely to go down if the market takes another hit. When shopping for dividend stocks in a bull market, I aim for the best combination of yield and P/E ratio that I can find.

If you were wondering whether it's permissible to purchase a stock between the time the company announces a dividend and the cutoff date for receiving it, the answer is yes. In fact, there's a dividend investment technique making the rounds on the internet called "dividend capture," where you're supposed to buy a stock immediately after the dividend is declared, take the dividend payout, and then turn around and sell it. It sounds good on paper, but it fails to take into account how dividends affect share prices. I tried this and immediately learned the drawbacks. First off, dividend share prices tended to go up immediately after the declaration date, because other investors were thinking just like me. Secondly, as soon as the ex-dividend date passes, the dividend amount is deducted from the share price, which effectively made my "capture" a wash. On top of that, I had to deduct my brokerage fees from both my purchase and my sale. Lesson learned: stock flipping isn't for me.

How to Buy Dividend Stocks

So you have done some research and you know which companies pay dividends, as well as their track record. You have set a budget for your investing activities and discussed it with anyone who will be affected by it, such as your spouse or partner. You have noted the share price for each of your picks, and you have decided how many shares of each you want to buy. You have weighed the pros and cons of building your portfolio yourself out of individual stocks, vs. investing in a managed fund and letting the fund manager build your portfolio for you. And you have evaluated the benefits of cash payouts of dividends vs. dividend reinvestment plans (DRIPs).

Let's say you have settled on individual stocks for now, and you have decided to accept your dividends as cash payments.

Your next move is to find a discount brokerage firm or an online brokerage and open an account. Deposit at least the required minimum of cash, or however much money you plan to invest. For an online brokerage, or a discount brokerage with online account management, you'll need to obtain your password and familiarize yourself with your dashboard on the company's website.

From here, buying and selling is simple: either call your discount broker, or use your online dashboard, and specify the number of shares you want for each company you are investing in. If you want to sell, the process is the same. You will want to be careful of running up brokerage fees each time you buy and sell, so make sure you plan your activities in advance, before you make that phone call or log in to your brokerage website. Be sure to learn the difference between a cash account and a margin account (see Chapter 7).

Dollar Cost Averaging

One way to smooth out the bumps in the market is to set up dollar cost averaging with your broker. With this strategy, you pick a set dollar figure to invest on a periodic basis, for example, every month, or every pay period. You can even arrange to have this amount automatically direct deposited in your brokerage account. You then commit to investing this amount no matter what. If the market is up, you'll buy more shares; if it's down, you'll buy fewer shares.

The drawback of dollar cost averaging is the brokerage fees you incur each time you make a trade. Trading once a week or once a month will eat away at your investment piggy bank while you lose out on the chance to invest the money you spend on fees. I have avoided it for that reason, with one exception: my dividend reinvestment plan, which doesn't incur fees each time I make a trade.

Managed Funds for Dividends

If you're building your dividend portfolio yourself with individual stocks, then you will need your broker to carry out your buy and sell orders. However, many investors choose to invest in managed funds and let the fund manager pick their stocks and handle the broker relationship. This is more of a challenge with dividend investing, which is highly individualized, but it's not impossible, and I'll explain how. But first, let me give you a quick summary of how managed funds work, and the different types.

Managed funds are promoted heavily by the finance industry as an entry portal for people with no investment background to get started in the market. They are popular with investors who want a more hands-off investing approach. Oversight of a managed fund is carried out by its board of directors or trustees, who hire the fund manager. The manager, who must be a registered investment advisor, buys and sells the fund's shares through a broker on behalf of the fund's investors, who are the shareholders in the fund.

Managed funds may be actively or passively managed:

- **Active management:** In an active fund, the manager examines the market and assembles a large portfolio of stocks that he or she believes will outperform the market average. The manager also trades regularly to maintain the robustness of the fund's income. Active management comes with a price, though. You, the investor, pay a management fee to the fund itself, and frequently the brokerage fees on all trading within the fund as well.

- **Passive management:** in a passive fund, the stocks simply track an objective metric, such as an index. They tend to have far more reasonable management fees because their individual stock makeup seldom changes, so there's no need for a highly-compensated fund analyst to pick stocks. Additionally, there are very few trades, so brokerage fees per trade stay very low.

Some advantages of managed funds are:

- Many investors are busy, or have no interest in the market, so they prefer to have someone else manage their portfolio for them.

- Managed funds provide investors with terrific portfolio diversity that would take time to duplicate by buying shares individually.

Some disadvantages of managed funds are:

- With actively managed funds, the aforementioned high fees are a major deterrent, because every dollar you sink into fees is one less dollar you can invest and make money with. Passively managed funds don't have this disadvantage.

- Research has shown that actively managed funds, particularly mutual funds, don't outperform the major indexes. In fact, in many cases, their performance was *worse*, mainly due to factoring in their high fees.

Here are some of the different types of managed funds.

Mutual Funds

A mutual fund is a company, usually a corporation, that pools shareholder money to buy securities, such as stocks, bonds, and other instruments, and sells shares of the company to the public. Some mutual funds are growth investment funds, while others provide their shareholders with income through distributions. The more shareholders the fund has, the more money it has available to invest. Investment decisions are made by a fund manager who makes strategic picks of stocks and other securities for the benefit of the fund's members – but without their input. Mutual funds may be actively or passively managed.

I've always preferred to pick my own stocks, so I don't invest in mutual funds – at least, not voluntarily. When my employer put all of its salaried professional staff into a "defined contribution" pension plan, I became a de facto mutual fund investor, like millions of other Americans.

Mutual funds often have trademarked names that describe the character of the securities they contain. For example, a fund might only invest in midsize company stocks, or Fortune 500 stocks, or energy sector stocks. Many funds are titled by their objective, such as rapid growth, or stable investment, or higher risk. If I were investing in a mutual fund, I would take the time and effort to wade the through the prospectus, even though it's not light reading, and learn as much as I can about the fund.

One thing I've learned from doing some research is that a number of mutual funds track the indexes pretty closely – so closely that they might more accurately be called index funds, except that mutual funds charge much higher fees!

If you've decided mutual funds are the right investment vehicle for you, then you'll be pleased to hear that a number of them specialize in dividend stocks. These funds will include the word "dividend" in the name of the fund, since that will be one of the fund's primary objectives.

Index Funds

An index fund is a special type of mutual fund made up of all stocks in a particular index. (An index, as I explained in Chapter 3, is a set of stocks that the index company chooses as representative of the entire stock market, such as the DJIA or the S&P 500.) Index funds are passively managed because there's no rocket science involved in picking stocks – the index fund company simply mirrors the stocks in the index. An index fund is more transparent than a mutual fund, because you can check its portfolio by looking at the index its based on.

Index funds combine the best features of both actively and passively managed funds. They're very diverse, because the indexes are diverse, and they're hands-off – you simply invest in the fund. However, unlike actively managed funds, their fees are very low, because the makeup of an index seldom changes, and there are no judgment calls to be made when picking stock. For this reason, index funds perform about as well as the overall market does.

Happily, index fund companies have recognized the value of dividend investing and are marketing dividend index funds by compiling all of the stocks in their index that pay dividends.

Exchange Traded Funds (ETFs)

An ETF mirrors a particular index, just like an index fund. The critical difference, though, is that ETFs trade on the stock exchange, while index funds are sold through financial management companies. To invest in an ETF, you check the share price of that fund, call your broker, and tell him or her how many shares you want to buy. Since ETFs are based on an index, they are passively managed, and they have all the diversity of an index fund.

Just like index funds, ETFs are available made up of dividend stocks only. Dividend ETFs have become a hot item in the investment world lately. There are plenty of options to choose from, so look at all the choices before you make your picks.

Dividend Reinvestment Plans (DRIPs)

A growing number of publicly traded companies that pay dividends are starting to offer dividend reinvestment plans (DRIPs) to their shareholders. When you enroll in a DRIP, your dividends are automatically applied to purchasing more stock for you in that company, instead going to you as a cash payout.

Most DRIP plans are managed directly, either by the company issuing the dividend-paying stock or by a low-cost transfer agent. Direct management allows you to bypass your broker and avoid brokerage fees. This is important because dividends are paid out in smaller dollar amounts than the actual price of the shares. If you had to go through a broker to reinvest your dividends, the brokerage fees could easily eat up your dividend money. In this respect, DRIPs are just like dollar cost averaging (see Chapter 5), but without the brokerage fees.

Brokerages also manage DRIP plans on behalf of companies. These plans incur transaction fees just like any other buying or selling you do through your broker.

DRIPs are unusual because they allow you to purchase fractions of a share, instead of requiring you to buy whole shares. The ability to purchase fractional shares makes the cost of entry very low for the beginning investor. I got started with DRIPs as soon as I learned about them, and my initial purchase cost me a whopping $25.

The "DRIP" acronym is appropriate here, because although

you're dealing in small amounts of money, DRIP growth is steady over time. Each quarter when a company pays a dividend, you end up owning more shares of dividend-paying stock in that company, and in the next quarter, those new shares also will pay out dividends – which the DRIP uses to buy yet more stock. The effect is exactly like compounded interest, as more and more shares "drip" into your portfolio and pay for the purchase of even more stock.

Are there any drawbacks to DRIPs? I can think of a few:

- **Tax treatment:** even though your dividend income is reinvested, it's still taxed as income when the dividend is paid out.

- **Liquidity issues:** buying and selling stock through a broker is fast and easy. Getting your money out of a DRIP takes a few weeks and in many cases is restricted to quarterly intervals. You also may pay a fee to withdraw.

Making Your Move with a DRIP

Here are the steps for investing in a DRIP. If you're new to the market and don't have a brokerage account, you'll need to do a bit of extra work at the beginning.

The first step for investing in a DRIP is to find the company whose shares you want to invest in, make sure they pay dividends, and make sure the DRIP plan is available directly through that company or a transfer agent. The easiest way to find out is to go to that company's website and search its investor section. Companies like Coca-Cola, Verizon, and General Electric offer DRIPs to their shareholders. Many large-company DRIPs are managed by ComputerShare,:
http://www.computershare.com/us/Pages/default.aspx, a well-known transfer agent. Go to the investor center section and take a look at what various companies require to get started.

Next, you must purchase a minimum of one share of that company's stock. If you already have a brokerage account, you can just have your broker buy the share for you if you don't own it already. (Note: this doesn't mean you're investing in a brokerage-managed DRIP; it's just the easiest way to buy a single share). If you don't have a brokerage account and don't have the funds to make the minimum deposit to open one with a discount broker, then a quick web search for online brokers will present you with several options for getting that coveted first share cheap. Choose one that doesn't charge a setup fee or require a minimum deposit.

After that, you need to become the shareholder of record. When you buy a share through a brokerage, the brokerage is the shareholder of record, so you need to ask them to transfer the stock certificate to you. Keep in mind that this can take a week or two, and that there might be a fee. Before you choose an online broker, make sure they can do this for you before you commit, and that the fee is reasonable.

Finally, go back to the transfer agent website, fill out the application, and submit it. Follow their instructions and wait for them to send you verification that you're enrolled in the DRIP. Don't forget that all this takes days, and sometimes weeks.

Real Estate Investment Trusts (REITs)

After the collapse of the housing bubble in 2008 (see Chapter 10, Spotlight: The 2008 Collapse of the Financial Market and the Fate of the Big Banks), real estate wasn't very popular as an investment vehicle because people lost a lot of money. However, experience has taught me that time always sorts out the winners and losers. Since then I've gradually started adding real estate to my portfolio, but only in the form of Real Estate Investment Trusts (REITs). I invest in these securities for both growth and income. Done right, they can result in capital appreciation over time, plus they pay out dividends. Many of them are available in a DRIP as well.

An REIT is a managed fund that invests in the real estate market directly and trades its shares on a stock exchange. The concept is very similar to an ETF and features the same advantages. Investors get good portfolio diversity like a mutual fund, but they can buy and sell their shares through their broker. An additional advantage of REITs, and the major one in my opinion, is that they're a way to invest in the real estate market while keeping my money liquid. If I were to directly invest in real estate, I would have to raise huge amounts of money to buy an entire property, and the only way to get my money out would be to sell that property. With REITs, I can invest as little or as much money as I want, and investing that money elsewhere is a simple matter of calling my broker.

How is the payout for REITs? In my experience, pretty good. Because of the special laws governing REITs, they tend to pay out at least 90 percent of their profits to shareholders in order to receive favorable tax treatment, so they often have higher yields than other investments. However, I always keep in mind that real estate is a volatile market at this time and losses are a real possibility. I do a lot more research before investing in a REIT than I would for, say, an index fund.

Some REITs are owners of physical real estate properties and act as landlords. Typically these are commercial properties, such as shopping malls or golf courses. Property REITs also may be bundled by geographical location, so you can pick them based on how well the real estate market is doing in a particular area.

Another type of REIT invests only in real estate mortgages. Since lending standards have tightened since 2008, I've become more comfortable with this type of REIT. Some REITs invest in both physical properties and mortgage securities.

REITs are also available in the form of mutual funds for investors who prefer to invest through a financial manager instead of via a brokerage firm.

The tax treatment for REITs may not be as favorable as for other investment vehicles. Your income from an REIT may be taxed at the ordinary income rate. Be sure to consult your tax professional before   you   make   this   investment.

Chapter 10
Looking Toward the Future

Whether you're a cautious buy-and-hold investor or a short-term trader, I hope this book has inspired you to make a commitment to the art of investing for the long haul. As you learn more and refine your investment strategy, you'll find that the rewards increase – both financial and personal.

The IRS and the Stock Market

Although a complete rundown of the tax issues surrounding investment would be a book in itself, below I lay out the primary concerns that you and your accountant should have as you figure your taxes on your investments. For simplicity's sake, I've limited my summary to US tax policy, which can be found on the IRS website http://www.irs.gov

Capital Gains Tax

You realize capital gains on your stocks when you sell them at a higher price than you paid for them, and you'll be liable for taxes on the difference. Note that as long as you hold the stock, you're not liable for taxes on it even if it appreciates in value – it's only when you sell that the IRS considers you to have made a profit on your investment.

IRS tax policy favors long-term investment, which is one of the reasons a buy and hold strategy is popular with investors. If you hold a stock for more than one year before selling it, your capital gains tax will be 15% or 20%, depending on your tax bracket. If your income is less than $400,000 (single), or $450,000 (married couples), you pay 15%. If your income is over these amounts, you'll pay 20% capital gains tax plus the health care surtax of 3.5%.

If you hold your stocks for less than one year, your capital gains are taxed at the rate of ordinary income, which tends to be around 30%.

Taxation of Dividends

The IRS does not consider dividend payments to be capital gains, so it taxes them as ordinary income.

The tax formulas for dividends can be complex, but the basic rate is simple enough. Since companies figure their dividends based on their after-tax profit, you benefit from the fact that Uncle Sam has already taken his slice of the pie.

Dividends are divided into two categories. "Qualified" dividends are taxed at a graduated rate, depending on your tax bracket, just like capital gains. "Qualified" dividends are taxed at either 0%, 15%, or 20%. To qualify, the company must be headquartered in the US (or have a treaty agreement with the US that the IRS accepts), and you must hold the stock for more than 60 days during the 121-day period that begins 60 days before the ex-dividend date (see Chapter 8). "Unqualified" dividends are taxed as ordinary income. Since these rates are a vestige of the "Bush tax cuts," which Congress has extended for short intervals after they officially expired in 2010, they could change again in the near future.

Most dividends stocks are qualified, but one way to make them unqualified is not owning them long enough. In my ill-fated experiment with dividend capture (see Chapter 9), I got nailed for the maximum tax rate because I didn't own the stock long enough to qualify for the reduced rate.

Taxes on Interest

If you invest in bonds or other debt securities that pay interest, you must declare the annual interest on them, even if they haven't reached maturity yet. There's one happy exception, though, and that's most municipal bonds. These bonds feature "triple tax-free" status – that is, their interest earnings are exempt from federal taxes, as well as the state and local taxes in the state and locality where they are issued (see Chapter 1, Spotlight: The Detroit Bankruptcy of 2013 and the Fate of the Muni Bond).

Finding the Right Accountant

My accountant has been a big help to me with investing. I strongly recommend that you consult yours, and if you don't have one, start asking friends and family for recommendations. The phone book isn't a good way to go about finding an accountant – if you find the right one for you this way, you're just lucky. The ideal accountant for you is one who understands not only the tax laws regarding investment, but the unique needs of the serious retail investor. The best way to find one is to talk to other investors who are at the same level as you or slightly above.

If you don't know anyone like this in your local community, then social media sites online are probably your next stop. Two of them that cater to retail investors are LinkedIn.com and Meetup.com, both of which have numerous investment groups with active conversations about various investment topics. Some of them, particularly on Meetup, may be located in your community, making it easy to ask for referrals. Be sure to do your due diligence if you go this route. Online communities have distinct personalities, often determined by who the movers and shakers are in that particular group. Spend some time just observing before you jump in so you can make sure the information and its sources are credible. Your broker, if you have a good relationship with him or her, can be another source of referrals.

Although there are various categories of financial professionals, I believe there's no substitute for retaining a Certified Public Accountant if you're serious about your investments. The training they receive is rigorous, and many of them tailor their businesses for professional and amateur investors. The main question is whether to choose a large commercial accounting firm, or an independent CPA. My experience has been that an independent is more likely to understand me as an independent investor, but it's also true that the large firms have more resources available for their CPAs in terms of training and continuing education. Either way, make sure your CPA is a member of the American Institute of Certified Public Accountants (AICPA), which requires continuing education credits in order to maintain membership.

I interviewed three CPAs before settling on the one I've been with since my second year of investing. My interview questions centered around accessibility, cost, and the intangible quality of personality.

- **Accessibility**: I made sure that if I called with a financial question, I'd be able to talk directly to my accountant and not get shunted off to support staff. Obviously staff can answer very basic questions about things like deadline dates, but if it concerns my investments, I want to talk to directly to the financial professional that I have an ongoing relationship with. If you're interviewing someone at an accounting firm, make sure you'll be talking to him or her each time you call, and not rotated around to various CPAs.

- **Cost:** A good accountant won't mind discussing fees with you. Don't settle for someone who has an attitude of, "If you have to ask, you can't afford it." However, don't be put off if good accounting services cost more than you expect. You're paying for a lot more than just a basic tax service. Just make sure you're getting good value for your money.

- **Personality:** There are plenty of good accountants out

STOCK MARKET INVESTING MADE PLAIN

there, so take a little extra time to find one that you "click" with, someone who is supportive of your investment goals and activities. Although an accountant isn't the one to tell you which stocks are winners, you're looking for someone who has a tolerance for risk that roughly matches your own. It's just easier when you're both on the same page.

Whatever you do, expect that a potential CPA will let you take 30 minutes or so to conduct the interview free of charge. You're looking at a long-term relationship, so you shouldn't be expected to pay for simply doing your due diligence.

Foreign Investment

As the US economy continues to confound the experts with its volatility and sluggish economic indicators, many investors are turning to foreign markets as a source of diversification and better returns. In the past, foreign investment was only for the experts, but today you can find a wealth of mutual funds and ETFs that focus on international securities. These conventional investment vehicles are no harder to buy than their domestic counterparts. However, you still have to learn as much as you can about these new markets before you commit your investment dollars.

One advantage of foreign assets is that they are **uncorrelated** – that is, they aren't all tied to the same market, so they change value independently of one another. Sure, you can diversify in the US market, but ultimately you'll still be tied to the US economy, which hasn't been turning in inspiring performances lately, no matter which sector you invest in. Foreign markets just might be the ultimate diversification strategy.

At the same time, keep in mind that most blue-chip stocks on the US exchanges have substantial foreign operations and revenues. The good news is that, rather than being tied to the US economy, these companies are able to realize substantial gains from the global economy, even when the domestic economy is turning in a

130

LOOKING TOWARD THE FUTURE

sluggish performance. When conducting a fundamental analysis of a company you're considering investing in, one additional question to ask might be, "What level of globally diversified earnings does it have?"

Many foreign economies are thriving in ways that the US only dreams of. Investors have lavished significant attention on Brazil, Russia, India and China, collective known as "BRIC." These countries have emerging economies and are seeing economic growth, so they're worth paying attention to. However, all four of them are developing nations, so investments are not without risk. Here are some of the risks that go hand in hand with investing in developing countries.

- **Credit risks:** Despite its problems, the US has managed to maintain its AAA credit rating through upturns and downturns. Other countries might not be as solid. Other countries may also be more vulnerable to economic changes than countries with economies that have been stable over the long term.

- **Currency exchange risks:** The value of the US dollar fluctuates against the value of other currencies on a daily basis. Activity in the financial markets can affect the exchange rate and wipe out your gains without any other changes taking place.

- **Political risks:** One look at the news will tell you that political instability is a fact of life in many parts of the world. Even if a country has a stable government, a bellicose neighbor can pose a threat that might affect its neighbors' financial standing.

Despite the risks, investing abroad presents a whole new set of opportunities and challenges as the trend toward globalization continues and emerging economies take their place in the investment world. Just remember: although things change quickly in the US market, they can change far more quickly overseas.

Planning for the Future

With the knowledge you gain from this book, you're ready to develop your one-year, five-year, and 10-year investment plans. The journey begins with setting your investment goals and determining your resources. One resource that's often ignored in the financial literature is time. Although building your own portfolio is a pleasure and a challenge, the reality may be that you just don't have enough hours in your week to do the necessary research. Although there's no set figure of hours per week per stock, I've found that devoting four or five hours a week to fundamental analysis has allowed me to build a portfolio of 20 to 30 individual stocks over a period of a year. Of course, professional investors spend far more time than this, but that's why they're professionals.

If you're making your picks with the long term in mind, you should be able to obtain all of your research data for free over the internet. Day traders need real time data directly from the floor, but if you're not flipping stocks, a good online source of charts is sufficient. For financial statements, the SEC's Edgar database is a rich source of data for fundamental analysis (see Chapter 5). Don't neglect the company's own website, which is probably the best source of qualitative analysis data you can get.

Consider setting some benchmark figures to streamline your search. If you don't select a cutoff range for numbers like market cap or valuation, you'll find yourself literally surveying the entire market – a sure-fire recipe for burnout. A good stock screener tool like the one on Yahoo! Finance (see Chapter 8) can make this job so much easier. You won't find yourself getting distracted by too much information because the tool screens it out so you never see it.

Consider streamlining the process of diversification by investing in exchange-traded funds (ETFs). The sector ETFs (see Chapters 3 and 4) are especially good for allocating your investment funds to certain sectors without going through the work of screening each individual stock. If you want to develop an expertise in a certain sector, you can always buy ETFs (or even mutual funds) in the other sectors and then focus on individual stocks in the area you want to become an expert in.

Keep a "tickler file" of stocks to watch. Sometimes the valuation isn't quite right, or you simply don't have time to do a complete review of the company. With a weekly review of this list, you can stay current with companies that might become a good value, and you'll have a ready supply of potential replacements when you sell a stock.

Adopt a strategy of reviewing your allocations regularly. Be mindful of stability (or instability) in the market and decide whether you want to move in the direction of less risk, or more. You can also move your investment dollars into or out of managed funds such as ETFs and mutual funds, depending on your current level of expertise and your available supply of time.

Finally, enjoy the journey as well as the destination. There will be a learning curve, and you're going to see some losses as well as gains. Be cautious in the beginning and then give yourself greater latitude as you learn more and gain confidence. Think of your learning process the same way you think of your investments: in terms of years, not weeks or months. Make your learning process constant, and you'll find that investing is a source of personal as well as financial satisfaction over time.

SPOTLIGHT: THE 2008 COLLAPSE OF THE FINANCIAL MARKET AND THE FATE OF THE BIG BANKS

When investors look back on the period leading up to the financial crisis of fall 2008, the word "bubble" comes up frequently. The run-up to the crisis featured historic highs for stock prices, big profits for realtors and lenders, and homeowners treating their houses like ATM machines via home equity loans. When the bubble collapsed, it triggered the worst crisis in the US financial markets since the Great Depression and sent shock waves throughout the world economy. The major financial markets lost more than 30 percent of their value, and the fallout from the crisis still lingers more than six years later, even though the stock market has rebounded once again to record highs.

The collapse wasn't a surprise to everyone. Howard Marks, for example, dubbed it a "race to the bottom" in 2007 (see Chapter 6, Building Your Portfolio: How the Experts Do It), and many experts had cautioned long before the Great Recession (as it came to be called) that the subprime mortgage market was a house of cards destined to fall. The beginning was in 1999, when the Federal National Mortgage Association (Fannie Mae for short) began lending to the subprime market to encourage home ownership. The borrowers typically had less-than stellar credit and less cash to pony up for a down payment, or they were self-employed in volatile industries like tech and couldn't provide proof of steady income.

These subprime loans were also attractive for private mortgage lenders, who could charge higher interest rates and get very creative in structuring variable repayment plans. These lenders took over where Fannie and Freddie left off, serving the riskiest clientele, and writing very large mortgages that the government-backed agencies couldn't touch due to legal limits on loan amounts. The housing market responded to the huge influx of available mortgage money as any self-respecting supply and demand market would – home prices went up, up, and away.

As long as prices kept going up, everyone was happy. The private lenders found a home for their loans in the mortgage-backed securities (MBS) market. The MBS investment vehicle pooled bundles of mortgages together into single securities and sold them in the private securities market. Purchasers of these securities could collect the premiums and interest on each individual mortgage, which worked out swimmingly as long as the borrowers actually kept paying on their notes. A similar scenario occurred with credit default swaps (CDSs), which divided mortgages into smaller pieces called tranches, combined them, and traded them, allowing buyers of these securities to spread the risk of default even thinner than the MBS market by widening the pool.

The coup de grace occurred in early 2008 as the creative repayment schedules in the private lending market started hitting maturity. Adjustable rate mortgages (ARMs) with reset periods as low as three years meant that borrowers saw their monthly payments doubling or even tripling. As long as property values stayed high, over-leveraged borrowers could simply flip their way out of the old loan, either by refinancing, or by selling the house and buying a newer, usually more expensive one. But the easy mortgage lending environment meant that the housing market was overbuilt, with thousands of new homes in pricey development projects sitting empty. Again, under the law of supply and demand, the glut of housing stock meant that prices started to fall – but the homeowner's mortgage debt obligations didn't. This resulted in a wave of defaults as homeowners went "underwater" and got stuck with houses they couldn't sell for as much as they owed for them.

All this was taking place right after the total consumer debt in the US hit an astonishing $2 trillion for the first time in history due to consumers relying on credit card debt to finance their lifestyles, and, as their ARMs reset, simply to pay their bills. In 2007, Bear Stearns was first investment bank to fail due to the collapse of the subprime lending market; it was bought out by JP Morgan Chase. The failure of IndyMac bank (formerly Countrywide Mortgage, which was arguably the heaviest hitter in the subprime market) in summer 2008 was a harbinger of what was to come. Foreclosures and bankruptcies ramped up, and in highly leveraged cities like Las Vegas, empty foreclosed homes stood row upon row. By this time, hundreds of thousands of mortgages had been sold, resold, sliced and diced so many times that in many cases no one was sure who actually owned them.

Oddly enough, the stock market remained untouched as of October 2007, with the Dow closing above 14,000; but by summer 2008 it fell to 11,000, and it would fall further. In fact, on October 10, 2008, it hit a shocking low of 7,882. Meanwhile, the S&P 500 fell more than 50 percent between October 2007, at 1,576, to March 2009, when it plummeted to 676. Everyone took a bath, from professional investors, to serious retail investors, to ordinary people with their retirement money tied up in mutual funds.

The period of late September to early October 2008 was an especially wild ride. Lehman Brothers, the second major investment bank to fail, filed for bankruptcy on September 14 because of its losses in the subprime mortgage sector, and kicked the bottom out of the financial markets. Because Lehman held so much commercial paper in the money market, its failure touched off a panic and started a run on the money market, with holders scrambling to get their money back.

Only a few days later, more dominoes fell, as the brokerage giant Merrill Lynch was bought out by Bank of America (which had already acquired the defunct Countrywide), and American International Group (AIG) got a downgrade in its credit rating. Washington Mutual also failed that month, with JP Morgan Chase acquiring its assets – and its losses. In all, 130 banks failed and fell under FDIC control during 2008-2009, which put major stress on the agency's reserves.

The Troubled Asset Relief Program (TARP) was first discussed at the US Treasury on September 18, 2008. Even the mere discussion of a federal bailout brought some relief to the market, but it would be early October before the $700 billion bailout gained enough bipartisan support in Congress to pass. When the dust had cleared, only four big banks were left standing: Wells Fargo, Citigroup, and the aforementioned JP Morgan Chase and Bank of America. None of the big four was as big as it used to be, though.

As for the investors who held on for the ride when the market went into freefall, the old adage that stocks can't keep falling forever held true. In February 2013, the Dow hit 14,000 for the first time since 2007, which was some help in restoring investor confidence. But although the indexes had regained their old luster, that didn't necessarily hold true for individual stocks. There were many, many casualties of the Great Recession. Most of them were small companies, but the fallout reached all the way up to the blue-chip giant General Motors, which had once been considered nearly as safe as putting your money in a savings account.

My takeaway from the events of the great bear market of 2007-2009 is that when Wall Street is obviously over-leveraged, it's a good idea to park your money in a safe place until the storm is over, even if that means missing out on some returns. In all, the experience served as a sobering reminder of the investor's mantra: no reward without risk.